# THE CHURCH'S BEST-KEPT SECRET

## A Primer on Catholic Social Teaching

**New City Press**
Hyde Park, New York

The social teaching of the Catholic Church shows how universal the faith really is, touching all people regardless of age, social status, or ethnicity. By introducing us to this social teaching Mark Shea has invited all Catholics to deepen their faith in practical ways, and to put aside individualism and tribalism and open their hearts to everyone just because they are fellow human beings.

– **Bishop Thomas Dowd**, auxiliary of Montreal

In *The Church's Best-Kept Secret*, Mark Shea provides a faithful and spirited overview of Catholic social teaching grounded in Scripture, Vatican II, and papal writings since Leo XIII. He clearly explains the key principles of Catholic social teaching–human dignity, the common good, subsidiarity, and solidarity–and he shows that some Catholics, while rightfully opposing abortion and euthanasia, mistakenly reduce Catholic teachings on capital punishment and the environment to mere "prudential judgments" that can be ignored or opposed.

– **Robert Fastiggi**, Ph.D. Professor of Systematic Theology, Sacred Heart Major Seminary, Detroit, Michigan

In *The Church's Best-Kept Secret*, Mark Shea has written an accessible and essential primer for anyone interested in learning about Catholic teaching on human dignity and the common good rooted in the Gospel and Sacred Tradition. Transcending politics and ideology, this book provides a comprehensive overview of the Church's Magisterium on social issues, explaining how they are all interconnected, and why our moral decisions and actions have wide-ranging consequences.

– **Mike Lewis**, Managing Editor, *Where Peter Is*

Mark Shea has a gift for making official Catholic teaching accessible in a manner that displays not only its truth but also its beauty. In *The Church's Best-Kept Secret*, he shows that Catholic social doctrine challenges us to go beyond "liberal" and "conservative" distinctions. I recommend this book for all who seek to understand the fundamental principles behind that doctrine and apply it to their everyday lives, including their spiritual lives.

– **Dawn Eden Goldstein**, S.Th.D., theologian and author of *My Peace I Give You: Healing Sexual Wounds with the Help of the Saints*

In an increasingly polarized Church and world, we are accustomed to apologias and manifestos, jeremiads and rants. The word "catechesis" means to echo or resound and this resonance must be pastoral, in the voice of the Good Shepherd. Mark Shea captures this catechetical tone and pastoral spirit, eschewing polemics and hyperbole. His book echoes Catholic Social Teaching from our mother and teacher, the Church. It is a resounding success.

– **Samuel D. Rocha**, Associate Professor, University of British Columbia

# THE CHURCH'S BEST-KEPT SECRET

## A Primer on Catholic Social Teaching

### Mark P. Shea

Published by New City Press
New City Press
202 Comforter Blvd.
Hyde Park, NY 12538

www.newcitypress.com

Cover design and layout: Miguel Tejerina

ISBN: paperback: 978-1-56548-118-3
ISBN: e-book: 978-1-56548-127-5

Library of Congress Control Number: 2020939045

To Pope Francis,
who has preached Good News to the poor.


And to Servant of God Dorothy Day and Peter Maurin
who saw far, fought hard for the least of these,
ran the race, and won the crown imperishable.
Ora pro nobis!

# Contents

# Acknowledgments

Thanks above all to God, the Father, Son and Holy Spirit, from whom, to whom and through whom this book and all things exist. Blessed be he!

Thanks also to Janet, my wife, for all her love and support. Also, to our sons and grandchildren!

In addition, endless thanks go to:

All my readers at my old blog *Catholic and Enjoying It* and my new blog *Stumbling Toward Heaven*, as well as on Facebook and Twitter, and all who wanted me to write this project.

My supporters at Patreon.com.

Brian Warn, whose enthusiastic support for this project meant so much.

Sherry Weddell, whose friendship and support have blessed me so deeply over the years.

Nina Butorac, Charlie Camosy and John Médaille, whose helping critiquing and editing the manuscript was invaluable.

Deacon Steven Greydanus, for friendship, moral and spiritual support, and film tips.

Austen Ivereigh, for his help incorporating the teaching of *Laudato Si'* into this book.

The *National Catholic Register*, which published the original series of articles I wrote on Catholic Social Teaching that became the basis of this book.

Claude Blanc, who believed in this project and helped make it a reality.

The people of Blessed Sacrament parish in Seattle, Washington, and the folks at St. Pius X parish in Mountlake Terrace.

Also, special thanks to Saints Jerome, Athanasius, Anthony of the Desert, Francis de Sales, Dominic, Tertius, and, of course, Mama Mary, on whose constant intercession I rely for help. Ora pro nobis.

## Introduction

# The Church's Best-Kept Secret

*He has showed you, O man, what is good;*
*and what does the LORD require of you*
*but to do justice, and to love kindness,*
*and to walk humbly with your God?* – Micah 6:8

I once spoke about Catholic Social Teaching at a parish. On one side of the room sat the parish's Pro-life group. On the other side sat the parish's Peace and Justice group. Neither saw themselves as having anything in common with the other. Yet the whole point of my talk was that in the mind of the Church, which is the mind of Christ (see 1 Corinthians 2:16), both are part of the same Body, engaged in the same salvific mission to the world.

How did they not see that? Thereby hangs a tale.

## Thinking Beyond the Categories of the World

Some think of Catholic moral teaching in terms of the private and personal (and, for the most part, sexual). So for many, the Church should focus on so-called "Non-Negotiable teaching" (first and foremost, abortion and, to a lesser degree, euthanasia). Those with such a perspective tend to place on a lower rung Catholic teaching about more public issues such as taxation, workers' rights, poverty, immigration, politics, public spending, climate change, technology, health care, war, torture, gun violence, racism, or the death penalty. For them such issues are 1) a distraction from the Non-Negotiables, 2) politically "liberal," and 3) subject to "prudential judgment," a term which is commonly understood to mean "doing as we like."

Conversely, others think the Church should focus on these very public issues affecting billions of people around the globe. To them, the primary mission of the gospel is to create a just society in which the stranger, the orphan, and the widow are cared for and just structures are established to shield the vulnerable from the rich, powerful, and privileged predator. These folks sometimes regard the Church's teaching on our sex lives as a distraction from these issues.

Each group tends to like *some* aspects of the gospel, but each also tends to think there are areas where the Church should mind her own business. And (mark this) each therefore tends to evaluate the Church's social teaching in light of their political and cultural priorities rather than evaluating their political and cultural priorities in light of the Church's teaching. Consequently, they wind up on opposite sides of the room, darting suspicious glances at each other. Worse, they dart suspicious glances at the riches of the Tradition itself.

The trouble, very simply, is that a gaggle of warring voices in our culture assails us, urging us to think not with the mind of Jesus Christ, but with our favorite news vendor, or political party, or TV show, or pundit, or folk hero, or social media mini-pope, or circle of peers. The result is that actual Catholic teaching on how to order our common life remains the Church's best-kept secret.

That's not because the Church hides it. It is there in plain view in the *Compendium of the Social Doctrine of the Church*[1]—and more especially in the words of Jesus Christ himself. Rather, it is nearly invisible because the gospel is eternally at cross purposes with all those voices in our culture that are so much louder than the Church. So we are taught by our culture to ask, "Is it political, progressive, conservative, spiritual, left, right, modern, ancient?" but not "Is it in accord with what Jesus taught?" It is rather like when Jesus asked his apostles, "Who do people say that I am?" and got a wide diversity of opinions and guesses in response (see Matthew 16:13-14). The Church's moral teaching is regarded with tremendous confusion, not because it is confusing but because we are confused.

## Thinking with the Mind of Christ

So who is right? Should we care more about private, personal "pelvic" morality or primarily focus on what is popularly called "social justice" issues like poverty, racism, crime, and so forth? The answer of the Christian tradition is "Yes."

---

1.  Hereafter referred to as *Compendium* and available on-line at http://www.vatican.va/roman_curia/pontifical_councils/just-peace/documents/rc_pc_justpeace_doc_20060526_compendio-dott-soc_en.html as of September 25, 2019.

C.S. Lewis describes the Christian moral life this way:

There are two ways in which the human machine goes wrong. One is when human individuals drift apart from one another, or else collide with one another and do one another damage, by cheating or bullying. The other is when things go wrong inside the individual—when the different parts of him (his different faculties and desires and so on) either drift apart or interfere with one another. You can get the idea plain if you think of us as a fleet of ships sailing in formation. The voyage will be a success only, in the first place, if the ships do not collide and get in one another's way; and, secondly, if each ship is seaworthy and has her engines in good order. As a matter of fact, you cannot have either of these two things without the other. If the ships keep on having collisions they will not remain seaworthy very long. On the other hand, if their steering gears are out of order they will not be able to avoid collisions. Or, if you like, think of humanity as a band playing a tune. To get a good result, you need two things. Each player's individual instrument must be in tune and also each must come in at the right moment so as to combine with all the others.

But there is one thing we have not yet taken into account. We have not asked where the fleet is trying to get to, or what piece of music the band is trying to play. The instruments might be all in tune and might all come in at the right moment, but even so the performance would not be a success if they had been engaged to provide dance music and actually played nothing but Dead Marches. And however well the fleet sailed, its voyage would be a failure if it were meant to reach New York and actually arrived at Calcutta.

Morality, then, seems to be concerned with three things. Firstly, with fair play and harmony between individuals. Secondly, with what might be called tidying up or harmonising the things inside each individual. Thirdly, with the general purpose of human life as a whole: what man was made for: what course the whole fleet ought to be on: what tune the conductor of the band wants it to play.[2]

The Catholic Tradition makes the startling claim that Jesus has revealed the way to this tripartite gift of healing for ourselves, love and justice among all people, and the ultimate and eternal happiness that we all seek. To find it though, we must "have this mind among yourselves, which was in Christ Jesus" (Philippians 2:5) since God reminds us "My thoughts are not your thoughts,/neither are your ways my ways, says the LORD" (Isaiah 55:8).

One of the marks of Jesus' teaching is that, just as he is the Word made flesh, so he expects us to both speak and

---

2. C.S. Lewis, *Mere Christianity*, (New York: HarperCollins, 1960), 71-72.

enflesh his words. For Jesus, faith and obedience to his Father are one just as he and the Father are one. Talking the talk without walking the walk is rejected by him, while living out his words is filled with the assurance of his blessing:

> "Why do you call me 'Lord, Lord,' and not do what I tell you? Every one who comes to me and hears my words and does them, I will show you what he is like: he is like a man building a house, who dug deep, and laid the foundation upon rock; and when a flood arose, the stream broke against that house, and could not shake it, because it had been well built. But he who hears and does not do them is like a man who built a house on the ground without a foundation; against which the stream broke, and immediately it fell, and the ruin of that house was great." (Luke 6:46-49)

So strongly does he insist on obedience over mere pious words that he even tells a story in which a rebellious-sounding son is the hero, while his pious-sounding brother is the villain:

> "What do you think? A man had two sons; and he went to the first and said, 'Son, go and work in the vineyard today.' And he answered, 'I will not'; but afterward he repented and went. And he went to the second and said the same; and he answered, 'I go, sir,' but did not go. Which of the two did the will of his father?" They said, "The first." (Matthew 21:28-31)

Note that the dichotomy is not between one who believed and one who acted. It is between one who shows what he really believes by obeying the Father and one who shows what he really believes by disobeying the Father. For we do not have a choice, in the end, between faith and no faith. We only have a choice between obedient faith in God or disobedient faith in what is not God. Our actions show Who or what our faith is really in. "For where your treasure is, there will your heart be also" (Matthew 6:21).

So Paul, while insisting that we are saved by God's grace through faith also tells us that he "received grace and apostleship to bring about the *obedience* of faith" (Romans 1:5 [emphasis mine]). In short, Jesus saves us by grace in order to transform us from disobedient sinners to obedient and eternally happy saints.

That is why Paul also tells us, "Work out your own salvation with fear and trembling; for God is at work in you, both to will and to work for his good pleasure" (Philippians 2:12-13).

And John summarizes this eminently practical theology this way:

> If any one says, "I love God," and hates his brother, he is a liar; for he who does not love his brother whom he has seen, cannot love God whom he has not seen. (1 John 4:20)

All this is simply a reiteration of what Jesus himself says are the two most fundamental commandments in the entire Bible:

"You shall love the Lord your God with all your heart, and with all your soul, and with all your mind. This is the great and first commandment. And a second is like it, You shall love your neighbor as yourself. On these two commandments depend all the law and the prophets." (Matthew 22:37-40)

In other words, if we do not obey the second commandment, we cannot obey the first.

The reason for this is twofold:

1. There is, by the nature of our relationship with God, nothing we can do for him for the very good reason that he is God and we are not. He needs nothing. Our very ability to choose or act or love or even exist at all is pure gift to us from him. So though God commands that we love him above all, the paradox is that he does not do so out of any need. God is perfectly happy from all eternity and overflows with love because he *is* love (see 1 John 4:8). Everything we have and are is pure grace.

2. Therefore, precisely *because* God is love, he wills us into being gratuitously so we can participate in his divine life of love. And since we cannot give him anything, he creates us in such a way that we can "pay it forward" by loving our neighbor with God's love. In short, to love our neighbor *is* to love God.

So Jesus identifies himself with our neighbor so strongly that what we do (or neglect to do) to our neighbor is what we do (or neglect to do) to Jesus. This is the point of the famous Parable of the Sheep and the Goats (see Matthew 25:31-46).

That parable is about the salvation of those outside the visible communion of the People of God. Note that this does not mean "outside the Church" but simply outside the *visible* Church. When both the Sheep and the Goats meet the King, they are *surprised*. Unlike disciples of Jesus who are aware they serve Jesus in their neighbor, neither the Sheep nor the Goats had the slightest idea Jesus was present in their neighbor. Both ask, "Lord, when did we see *you* hungry or thirsty or a stranger or naked or sick or in prison?"

Christians know loving our neighbor is loving Jesus and so bear a greater weight of responsibility if we ignore that duty and can rejoice more greatly when we do it since it pleases the Lord we love. But this does not mean that people with no knowledge of Jesus Christ are oblivious to (or exempt from hearing) the cry of the poor, the hungry, and the dispossessed. The Sheep in the parable do the right thing for the same reason a disciple of Jesus does it: *because it is the right thing.* They are not saved by hard work without God's grace. Rather their good deeds are prompted by the grace of God already at work in their hearts. Because at the end of the day, God is God and is not dependent on the level of our theological education to act by the power of the Holy Spirit. As Paul says:

> When Gentiles who have not the law do by nature what the law requires, they are a law to themselves, even though they do not have the law. They show that what the law requires is written on their hearts, while their conscience also bears witness and their conflicting thoughts accuse or perhaps excuse them on that day when, according to my gospel, God judges the secrets of men by Christ Jesus. (Romans 2:14-16)

Conversely, the Goats will not be helped at the Pearly Gates by the excuse, "Hey! I didn't realize it was *you* I left to starve, Lord! I just thought it was some nobody. If I had known it was you, I totally would have helped."

That is because there are, in the words of J. Budziszewski, certain things we "can't not know."[3] The proof of this is seen in an old Steve Martin routine in which he urges the audience to remember that if you ever find yourself on trial for murder, just tell the judge, "I forgot murder was a crime." You can't not know that murder is evil. Conversely, you can't not know that it is good to do the things the Sheep in the parable did for the least of these.

In short, justice—that is, giving to another what is his or her due—is not some special revelation given only to Christians, but is something all human beings, made in the image and likeness of God, both deserve and are expected by God (and their own consciences) to live toward others.

---

3.   See J. Budziszewski, *What We Can't Not Know* (San Francisco: Ignatius, 2011).

So although Catholics alone are bound to observe certain precepts because they have received special revelation (for example, "Honor the Lord's Day by attending Mass"), a great body of moral teaching "written on our hearts" applies to all human beings—believer or not—because *every* person is due justice, fair dealing, and so forth. And they are due these things even if they themselves do not know or believe that they are made in the image and likeness of God.

Because justice is the duty of all human beings to uphold, it is also therefore the duty of each of us to give the best we can to the common good. Therefore, it is the duty of Catholics to delve into the riches of our Tradition and share it with our neighbors so that they too can profit from it. That is what this book is about.

## Four Pillars

The good news is that Jesus has not left us on our own to try to figure out that Tradition. Rather, he has poured out gifts on his Church to help us both know and do his will for our neighbor in love. As he told the apostles, "He who hears you hears me" (Luke 10:16).

What the Church teaches about how to love our neighbor comes to us through two millennia of apostles, prophets, evangelists, pastors, teachers, saints, philosophers, thinkers, and reformers pondering the implications of Jesus' teaching and, what is more, living it out.

Catholic Social Teaching can be pictured as a throne sitting on four pillars. Just as a throne would tip over if each leg differed in length, so these pillars are equally important and equally emphasized by the Tradition. Or, if you prefer, they are like four notes forming a single chord. They are:

- The Dignity of the Human Person

- The Common Good

- Subsidiarity

- Solidarity

I propose that, for the duration of this little primer, we set aside all those clamoring voices in our culture, choose to listen to the Church's Tradition, and see how the liberating gospel of Jesus Christ, articulated by the Magisterium—that is, the bishops of the Church in union with the Pope stretching back to the apostles—speaks the truth that sets us free.

# Chapter 1

# The Dignity of the Human Person: Made in the Image and Likeness of God

*Willy Loman never made a lot of money. His name was never in the paper. He's not the finest character that ever lived. But he's a human being, and a terrible thing is happening to him. So attention must be paid. He's not to be allowed to fall into his grave like an old dog. Attention, attention must finally be paid to such a person.*
– Arthur Miller, *Death of a Salesman*

When a child starves, or a veteran commits suicide after being deported by the country he served, or a poor mother is worked to death by two underpaying jobs, or a lunatic dictator starves his people, all who cry in outrage, "That's not the way it is supposed to be!" have in the back of their minds a notion, however dim, of the way it *is* supposed to be. The name for the "way it is supposed to be" is what the Church calls the *Dignity of the Human Person.* Just as you cannot know you are in the dark if you have never seen light, so you cannot perceive an insult to human dignity without believing human persons have dignity.

We feel and see the Dignity of the Human Person not only in the breach, but in the observance. We honor it when the humble are exalted, when a good man steps in to stop a bully picking on somebody weaker than himself, when a good woman does a thankless job so that a co-worker can visit her sick mother, when a child comforts her sad little brother. We feel it when George Bailey realizes his worth at the end of *It's a Wonderful Life*. We behold it in the face of a newborn child or a wise old woman.

Persons are due honor not because of their income bracket, looks, skin color, ancestry, intelligence, mental health, physical condition, age, citizenship, religion or lack thereof, sexual orientation, gender, or anything they do or don't do. They possess dignity for one reason only: because they are made—without any exception whatsoever—in the image and likeness of God. And it makes not one ounce of difference if that person believes in God or not: they still retain that dignity because of what they *are*. That is why a Catholic medical missionary in Africa, asked why she was treating Muslims, animists, and atheists in addition to Christian victims of Ebola, replied, "I don't treat people because they are Christian. I treat people because *I* am Christian."

The essential core of the Church's teaching concerning the Dignity of the Human Person can be sketched in twenty-four seemingly simple words:

> Human beings, made in the image and likeness of God, are sacred from conception to natural death and intended for eternal happiness with him.

This statement is founded on two crucial biblical truths. Let's take them one at a time.

## We are Made in the Image and Likeness of God

God created man in his own image, in the image of God he created him; male and female he created them. (Genesis 1:27)

Catholic teaching on the Dignity of the Human Person begins with the fact that creation—all of creation, but especially the creature called *Homo Sapiens*—is entirely *gratuitous*. Everything is a gift. Out of sheer love God both creates the universe—including us—and calls us to share in his divine life.

All authentic religious experience takes us toward this reality, which is why the Silver Rule ("Do not do to others what you would not have them do to you") and Golden Rule ("Whatever you wish that men would do to you, do so to them" (Matthew 7:21))—are universally recognized. Some try to deny this, but they always give away their game because they claim justice for themselves and complain if they are treated unfairly.

This primordial recognition of the moral law—what the Church calls "natural revelation"—is not the replacement for but the root of subsequent supernatural revelation. In the moral life, natural revelation is what your folks taught you about sharing with your sister, telling the truth, not hitting each other, being polite, cleaning up your messes and so forth.

Of course, ultimately even natural revelation comes from God since everything is his gratuitous gift, including those who taught you about common decency and cleaning your room. The Church tells us that these basic aspects of natural law are like the foundation of the house. Supernatural revelation builds on, not replaces, natural revelation.

Supernatural revelation begins with the call of Israel as God's Chosen People. Israel's expression of this primordial insight about the Dignity of the Human Person comes (as is typical for this ancient people) in imagery that is profoundly *liturgical*. So we see, for instance, in Genesis 1, a description of creation rooted in the liturgical imagery of Israel. Creation is pictured as the construction of a gigantic temple just as the Temple in Jerusalem likewise was festooned with decorations to recall Eden. And just as ancient temples had an image representing a god as the focal point, so the Temple of Creation built by God in Genesis has a divine image as well: man and woman—any man and woman, every man and woman.

The claim of supernatural revelation is not that we need God to tell us things our mother taught us, but that God is the grounding who helps us know why our mother was right—especially when we are strongly tempted to ignore her. And ignore her (and God) we have. All of us have sinned and fallen short of the glory of God (see Romans 3:23). That is what the story of the Fall of Man is about in Genesis 3. Individually and as a species, we have reached for the fruit of the Tree of the Knowledge of Good and Evil and therefore individually and as a species we are profoundly damaged by original sin: the loss of the divine life of God in the soul. That damage has resulted in warped and damaged behavior we call "actual sin." Consequently, we all experience the perennial temptation to reduce persons to things and exalt things above persons--which brings us to the next basic biblical fact.

## We Are All Sinners for Whom Christ Died

> God our Savior… desires all men to be saved and to come to the knowledge of the truth. (1 Timothy 2:3-4)

Many people have the idea that the Father is a schizophrenic, wrathful God who wants to damn us, yet who sent his Son Jesus so that in the Crucifixion he could pour out his wrath on him instead of us. In short, many people think *Jesus died to save us from his Father, not from our sins.*

This view of God has no foundation in Scripture nor in Catholic teaching. We are punished *by*, not *for*, our sins. God wills our salvation, not our damnation. He labors to save us from, not consign us to, our sins. The gates of Hell are barred *by us* from the inside, not by God locking us in against our will. Relatedly, according to the New Testament we, not God, were the authors of Christ's Passion. The apostles repeatedly say, "This Jesus whom *you* crucified… God raised from the dead" (Acts 4:10). God the Father wills our salvation and he has sent Jesus the Son and the Holy Spirit to bring it to us. The human race is not divided into those whom God wants to save and those he wants to damn. "The Church, following the apostles, teaches that Christ died for all men without exception: 'There is not, never has been, and never will be a single human being for whom Christ did not suffer'" (*Catechism of the Catholic Church*, 605).

So we are made in God's image and likeness, but also sinners capable of murdering God and each other as sin darkens our intellect, weakens our will, and disorders our desires. That's why we keep chasing after the four great idols of the human race—Money, Pleasure, Power, and Honor—instead of the love of God and neighbor. And as human history shows, individually and by the millions we will go to insane lengths to kill, conquer, enslave, exploit, torture, and experiment on others to get what we want.

That said, because our dignity comes from our nature—from the *kind* of creature we are—not from what we do, we retain our human dignity despite our sins. Because we can do nothing to earn the love of God, we can do nothing to lose it. God's response to our sin is not to hate us, but to turn even that sin into the means of our redemption. This does not mean "Let us sin that grace may abound" (see Romans 6:1-2). Nor does it mean that we cannot, for our part, cut ourselves off from God's constant offers of mercy, thereby putting ourselves in Hell. It means that God's purpose is *always* for our salvation because he is love.

And it leads to a maximalist, not minimalist, view of our obligation to seek the good of our neighbor that is, I would argue, the most significant development in Catholic doctrine of the past century.

## A Profound Development of Doctrine

Development of doctrine is a feature of the Catholic tradition dating back to the New Testament. Jesus likens the Church to a mustard seed (see Mark 4:30-32). Like every seed, when it begins it has the whole plant in potential. And like a seed, that potential unrolls and reveals itself as time goes on. The mark of *development*, as distinct from *mutation*, is that a developing thing becomes more itself, not less. So a mustard seed does not turn slowly into an octopus or a pine tree. It becomes more mustardy, not less. Likewise, a baby boy grows into a man, not a dog.

In the same way, over time Catholic teaching becomes more itself and the Church comes to understand its own teaching more profoundly as the Holy Spirit guides us into all truth (see John 16:13). You can see this process at work in Acts 15, for instance, as the Church confronts the question of whether Gentiles need to be circumcised and keep the ceremonial laws of the Old Testament (such as eating kosher, celebrating various feasts and Jewish liturgical rites, and so forth) in order to be saved. The Church realizes that the deeper meaning of these Old Testament symbols is to point to Jesus. Therefore, precisely because Jesus is here, Gentiles need not keep such rites. When you arrive at your destination, you don't need the map anymore. The paradox of this development is that the Church can appear to "reverse" herself while, in fact, she is drawing closer to the heart of God's revelation.

This is what took place at the Second Vatican Council. A new and still barely understood flower on the Mustard Plant bloomed and the Church fully clarified something that had always been latent, but had not been clearly articulated before. It was this: Man is, according to the Church, "the only creature on earth which God willed for itself."[4]

---

4. *Gaudium et Spes* 24 § 3. Available on-line at http://www.vatican. va/archive/hist_councils/ii_vatican_council/documents/vat-

The development was, in part, a response to the horrors of the 20th century in which human beings were radically subordinated to political, military, economic, scientific, religious, and philosophical systems that enslaved, degraded, and killed human beings by the millions. The Council's core insight was this: *No human being is a means to an end. No human being's good can be subordinated to some human system.*

The problem we face as we confront this development is that, as G.K. Chesterton said, "Men do not differ much about what things they will call evils; they differ enormously about what evils they will call excusable."[5]

Consequently, we are constantly tempted to bend or even break our principles concerning the Dignity of the Human Person out of fear or disordered love or some other distortion of the good. There is constant pressure from many different quarters to classify somebody or other as "not really" human or to say, in the words of George Orwell that, while all humans are equal, some are more equal than others. That is why Americans gave in to the sin of torture during the Iraq War: we were afraid and we decided we had to commit the grave and intrinsic evil of torturing prisoners to keep ourselves safe.

It's also why a significant portion of the population takes a tolerant attitude to abortion. Most people don't think it good any more than most people think torture

---

ii_const_19651207_gaudium-et-spes_en.html as of October 21, 2019.

5.    *Illustrated London News,* October 23, 1909

good. But about 60% of Americans, for instance, though they dislike abortion, don't want to oppose it because they find it "excusable." For them, the unborn are "less equal than others."

The Church says neither abortion nor torture is excusable, though both acts can be forgiven. Yet to say such things can be forgiven means they are real sins against the Dignity of the Human Person.

The point is this: because the human person is the only creature on earth whom God has willed for its own sake, there is no human person who can be thrown away for the sake of some other end. All human beings have equal dignity and value in the eyes of God. Their size, age, stage of development, class, color, gender, sexuality, work, crimes, and sin cannot remove, lessen, or increase the love of God for them any more than putting on sunglasses can cause the sun to shine less. This is why hair-splitting arguments about "when a fetus fully becomes a person" are meaningless. From a Christian perspective, it could well be argued that nobody fully becomes a person until they are saints in Heaven. But who would want *that* standard applied to them or somebody they love here on earth? Meanwhile, God loves every person into being and it is a waste of time to try to limit that love based on something as absurd as size or physical development. You might as well say a tall person is more valuable than a short one. So the Church, very rightly, insists that both abortion and infanticide are "abominable crimes" (CCC 2271) for the simple reason that they are the taking of innocent human life.

## Related, Not Opposed

More than this, the Church insists that the victims of these particular sins are profoundly *related* to the victims of other assaults on the Dignity of the Human Person, not *in opposition* to them. This is crucial, because nearly all of our political culture is founded on ideologies that are stone blind to that simple insight.

So, for instance, you will often hear people say things like "What's the point of worrying about a living wage when babies are being aborted?" (as though there is no relationship between not being able to afford a child and the fear that drives poor women to abort). We hear things like "What's the sense of talking about a 'right to health care' if you don't have the right to life?" (as though we cannot care about the unborn and the sick at the same time). We hear arguments like "Abortion is gravely and intrinsically immoral but capital punishment is not, so shouldn't we fight abortion and not the death penalty?" (as though the Church does not teach the sanctity of human life from conception to natural death even for the death row prisoner).

Conversely, we hear people say things like, "What's the point of people worrying about the rights of a blob of tissue? We should be worried about the rights of real people!" Again and again, the idea infecting those at either end of the spectrum is that the unborn are somehow the opposite of, not related to, all the other forms of human life God has made.

The Church's teaching on the Dignity of the Human Person comes back to one simple truth, constantly forgotten and constantly reasserted: every single human person, without exception, is made in the image and likeness of God and is to be protected and cherished from conception to natural death. No human person exists for the sake of some other end. Rather, all human systems are good only insofar as they contribute to the Dignity of the Human Person and they become evils the instant they assume priority over that. In short, the law was made for man, not man for the law (see Mark 2:27). Hold fast to that and you have the first and most foundational idea of Catholic Social Doctrine. Now let's talk about how that plays out in more detail in the Church's practical application of that teaching.

## Questions:

1. In your own words describe the biblical roots of the Church's teaching about the Dignity of the Human Person.

2. What are the principal challenges to that teaching in our culture?

3. What are some of the implications of the Church's teaching that man is the only creature on earth that God has willed for its own sake?

Chapter 2

# The Dignity of the Human Person: The Church's Consistent Life Ethic

*For truly, I say to you, till heaven and earth pass away, not an iota, not a dot, will pass from the law until all is accomplished. Whoever then relaxes one of the least of these commandments and teaches men so, shall be called least in the kingdom of heaven; but he who does them and teaches them shall be called great in the kingdom of heaven.* – Matthew 5:18-19

## Go Big or Go Home

As we mentioned in the previous chapter, the Church's teaching concerning the Dignity of the Human Person is maximalist, not minimalist. It seeks always to go big, not to skimp. Jesus tells us, "The thief comes only to steal and kill and destroy; I came that they may have life, and have it *abundantly*" (John 10:10). It is a mark of Hell to seek cheapness before all else, to find excuses to deprive people of life for the sake of some system. It is a mark of Heaven to seek that all people share in a riches of God abundantly and think nothing of the cost. So Paul tells us, "For you know the grace of our Lord Jesus Christ, that though he was rich, yet for your sake he became poor, so that by his poverty you might become rich" (2 Corinthians 8:9).

That is why a Consistent Life Ethic—which is to say the Catholic Life Ethic—defends all human life from conception to natural death without any exception whatsoever. It is not about trying to limit the provision of God to a select population of politically useful human beings. It is about *all* human beings. It is about the *right to live*, not merely the right to be born. "A right is a just claim. As we have duties and obligations toward one another, we also justly claim those rights which we inherit on account of our human nature, our human dignity."[6] It is about our dignity, not our usefulness, brains, or appearance. It is not even about sin, even if our sins are so grave that only God can forgive us. The Church defends the whole of human life for the whole of life.

Above all, the Dignity of the Human Person is about the *right to abundant life*: the right to reach the full potential of who and what God created each person to be and do. That means, in this life, not merely the right to the bare basics of human existence, but to sufficient food, shelter, health care, work, relations with other human beings, common respect, and love so that we meet our potential to the fullest. In the end, it is about the right of each human being to become the fullness of what God made that person to be: a saint. This is how C.S. Lewis describes the stakes for which we are playing:

---

6. Pope St. John XXIII, *Pacem in Terris*, I. 11, April 11, 1963. Available on-line at http://www.vatican.va/content/john-xxiii/en/encyclicals/documents/hf_j-xxiii_enc_11041963_pacem.html as of April 10, 2020.

It is a serious thing to live in a society of possible gods and goddesses, to remember that the
dullest and most uninteresting person you can
talk to may one day be a creature which, if you
saw it now, you would be strongly tempted to
worship, or else a horror and a corruption such
as you now meet, if at all, only in a nightmare.
All day long we are, in some degree, helping
each other to one or the other of these destina-
tions. It is in the light of these overwhelming
possibilities, it is with the awe and the cir-
cumspection proper to them, that we should
conduct all of our dealings with one another,
all friendships, all loves, all play, all politics.
There are no ordinary people. You have never
talked to a mere mortal. Nations, cultures, arts,
civilizations—these are mortal, and their life is
to ours as the life of a gnat. But it is immortals
whom we joke with, work with, marry, snub,
and exploit—immortal horrors or everlasting
splendors.[7]

Yet strangely, we now live in a time when more and
more Catholics are striving to limit the Dignity of the
Human Person to very specified groups while ignoring
many others. So, for instance, one Catholic pundit has
argued that, by "calling every issue a 'pro-life' issue, we
dilute and fracture the brand. We make other, less impor-

---

7.    C.S. Lewis, *The Weight of Glory* (New York: HarperCollins, 2009),
      45-46

tant issues as important as the abortion issue. We needlessly divide pro-lifers over prudential issues about which we should be able to respectfully disagree… As for me, I've come to realize that I'm no longer pro-life. Just call me anti-abortion."[8]

Such a view is foreign to the Magisterium of the Church, which demands "unconditional respect for and total dedication to human life from the moment of conception to that of natural death."[9] For the fact is, the Church's teaching, especially when it comes to the Dignity of the Human Person, is not either/or. It is both/and. More than this, the Church insists—and has done so since Paul wrote Romans 3:8—that we cannot do evil that good may come of it. We may, to be sure, try to *lessen* evil in an imperfect world without achieving perfection, but we cannot *deliberately choose to do evil* on the theory that our opposition to some other greater evil (like abortion) gives us a license to indulge an evil we are willing to tolerate.

This subtle distinction eludes many people, who have effectively embraced a theory of morality which holds that opposition to abortion taketh away the sins of the world. To get the hang of it, let us in this chapter take a look at

---

8.  Eric Sammons, "Why I'm Through Being Pro-Life", CatholicVote. org, July 9, 2018. Available on-line at https://catholicvote.org/ why-im-through-being-pro-life/ as of December 3, 2018.
9.  Pope St. John Paul II, *Ecclesia in America*, January 22, 1999. Available on-line at http://www.vatican.va/content/john-paul-ii/ en/apost_exhortations/documents/hf_jp-ii_exh_22011999_ ecclesia-in-america.html as of March 10, 2020.

the twenty-seven *other* things the Church teaches are issues pertaining to the Dignity of the Human Person in addition to abortion—many of them involving sins just as gravely and intrinsically evil—and see how they relate to—not oppose or compete with—the dignity of the unborn.

These issues tend to cluster around various forms of political, social, and economic violence in ways that are related, so we will take them in loose bunches, though each of them could easily be discussed on their own, and several of them could be grouped differently. However, the central point is that they are all, in one way or another, pro-life issues since they all pertain to the Dignity of the Human Person from conception to natural death.

## Issues Pertaining to War

War, torture, bodily mutilation, coercion of free will, violence, and murder are all named by Pope St. John Paul II as forms of assault on the Dignity of the Human Person. Of course, he did not cook up this list on his own (nor anything else we shall discuss hereafter). The Tradition has forbidden or tried to restrain such evils in various ways and at various times. Some are denounced in Scripture, others at later times, and some are particularly named in the documents of Vatican II. The reason is clear, just as the reason for *Evangelium Vitae*, the great 1995 encyclical on the Gospel of Life, is clear: because both the Council and the encyclical were, in no small part, responses to the massive 20th century assault on human life and the advances in technology and changes in thinking that made that assault possible.

Some of these evils are as old as Cain and Abel. But others involve social and technical refinements peculiar to modernity that have forced the Church to re-evaluate its tolerance of violence. The new phenomenon of the totalitarian state and of "total war," as well as the development of technologies enabling states to annihilate entire populations via weapons of mass destruction, or campaigns of genocide, or technologically enforced famines have changed the equation for the Church, and Just War Theory has required a great deal of rethinking.

The conditions of a Just War are these, according to the *Catechism* (2309):

- the damage inflicted by the aggressor on the nation or community of nations must be lasting, grave, and certain;

- all other means of putting an end to it must have been shown to be impractical or ineffective;

- there must be serious prospects of success;

- the use of arms must not produce evils and disorders graver than the evil to be eliminated. The power of modern means of destruction weighs very heavily in evaluating this condition.

The key point about Just War Theory is that it is designed as a series of *restraints* intended to make war as difficult as possible. And the issue facing the Church with the advent of modern warfare is simply this, according to Pope St. John Paul II:

Today, the scale and the horror of modern warfare – whether nuclear or not – makes it totally unacceptable as a means of settling differences between nations. War should belong to the tragic past, to history, it should find no place on humanity's agenda for the future.[10]

Pope Benedict XVI concurs with this and says that "given the new weapons that make possible destructions that go beyond the combatant groups, today we should be asking ourselves if it is still licit to admit the very existence of a 'just war.'"[11] In short, the Church—always skeptical about war and only indulging Just War Theory as a concession to human weakness—is now ratcheting forward to a place where she is increasingly suggesting that there may no longer *be* such a thing as a just war at all.

Some Catholics, confused about the meaning of Sacred Tradition, think that Just War Theory is a necessary feature of that Tradition. But this is not so. It is not essential to apostolic teaching and was only fashioned as a concession to human weakness in the centuries after the apostles. Even at its most robust, Just War Theory is specifically designed not to *bless* war, but to make it as hard as

---

10.  Pope St. John Paul II, *Pentecost Homily*, Coventry, UK, May 30, 1982. Available on-line at http://www.vatican.va/content/john-paul-ii/en/homilies/1982/documents/hf_jp-ii_hom_19820530_coventry.html as of December 3, 2019.

11.  "Challenging the Just War Theory" by Tony Magliano, *National Catholic Reporter*, September 1, 2014. Available on-line at https://www.ncronline.org/blogs/making-difference/challenging-just-war-theory as of December 4, 2019.

possible to permit—to throw a huge bucket of cold water on the fever, panic, vainglory, and bloodlust that typically precedes a civilization's plunge into war.

This explains some of the corollaries of the Church's teaching pertaining to war, such as her absolute forbiddance of torture as gravely and intrinsically immoral. One of the common arguments advanced in the first decade of the 21st century to rationalize America's use of torture was this: "If we get to kill people in war, then why shouldn't we get to torture them?"

The answer is that you don't *get* to kill people in war, you sometimes *have* to kill people in self-defense. But the moment enemy combatants become prisoners is the moment shooting them becomes murder, because they are made in the image and likeness of God. For the same reason, you can never torture them because violence is not a *privilege* of war, but a grim last-ditch necessity to be avoided whenever possible.

## Issues Pertaining to Socio-Economic Evils

The Church also lists arbitrary imprisonment, mistreatment of the environment, capital punishment, deportation, disease and lack of health care, drug abuse, hunger, poor working conditions, poverty, slavery, subhuman living conditions, and suicide as issues that affront the Dignity of the Human Person. There are a number of points worth touching on here since it is this collection of evils that brings us closest to what many see as "less important issues" than abortion that "dilute and fracture the brand."

The argument works, or seems to work, this way: Why should we spend time and energy on things like capital punishment or deportation or the fact that the United States is now a gigantic prison state when 1.5 million babies are dying each year? The same objection is typically advanced for nearly everything listed above. All these things are (goes the objection) "prudential judgments" and not gravely and intrinsically immoral as abortion is; therefore we can pass over them and, as the saying goes, "focus on abortion, which is non-negotiable."

But the problem with this approach, as the language about "diluting the brand" hints, is that the Church's teachings about these issues are not really passed over in favor of defending the unborn by those who use such language. On the contrary, the Church's teachings are *actively opposed by those who claim to, but do not, "focus on abortion."*

Here's the deal: There is plenty of room in the Church's tradition for specialization and focusing on specific issues, needs, and ills. Dominicans specialize in preaching. The Sisters of Providence specialize in healing and building hospitals. Jesuits found schools, and so forth. As Paul says, different members of the body do different things (see 1 Corinthians 12). So somebody who truly wants to focus on abortion and the protection of human life from conception to birth is perfectly free to do so.

But healthy members of the Body of Christ do *not* declare that other members "dilute the brand" by focusing on other issues or by caring about multiple issues at once. "The eye cannot say to the hand, 'I have no need of you,' nor again the head to the feet, 'I have no need of you'"

(1 Corinthians 12:21). Somebody who says "We need to address the sadistic cruelty being meted out to refugee children, snatched from their parents at the border and disappeared into a concentration camp system that cannot even figure out how to unite them with those parents again" is not "diluting the brand" of the Church's teaching, nor "distracting" from abortion. They are simply being consistent about the Dignity of the Human Person from conception to natural death.

Likewise, the person who is fighting to uphold the Church's teaching about the necessity of a living wage—a teaching as old as James 5 and the basis of the Church's tradition that depriving the worker of his wages is a sin that cries to Heaven for vengeance, exactly like murder—is not somehow "distracting" from abortion. Indeed, one crucial point of the Church's insistence on economic justice is that families cannot happen if people cannot afford to marry and have kids. Poverty, in fact, is the #1 abortifacient. A living wage is crucial to our dignity and to the foundation of families.

Another related issue is capital punishment. Recently, Pope Francis—echoing a call for the abolition of the death penalty also sounded by Popes St. John Paul II and Benedict XVI—formally changed the *Catechism* to read:

> Consequently, the Church teaches, in the light of the Gospel, that "the death penalty is inadmissible because it is an attack on the inviolability and dignity of the person," and she works with determination for its abolition worldwide. (CCC 2267)

This development definitively places the good of the human person over mere judicial retribution and says, in effect, that if we do not have to kill somebody we should not do it, even if they have it coming—especially since about 4% of our prison population (the largest on Earth) are wrongly convicted. Fighting this development in the Church's teaching not only means killing people unnecessarily, but killing innocents in order to do it and (no small thing as well), turning ourselves into people who are willing to kill innocents in order to kill the guilty unnecessarily.

"But these are all prudential judgments," returns the Focus-on-Abortion interlocutor. "Aren't we free to disagree with the Church on prudential matters?"

Actually, no. We are not free to ignore, or worse, oppose the Church's guidance without very grave cause. It is vital to remember that "prudential judgment" concerns not *whether*, but *how best* to implement the Church's *whole* teaching. If your focus is on abortion, fine. Focus on it. But do not *pretend* to focus on it while actually spending your time and energy fighting *against* the Magisterium and in favor of capital punishment, fighting *against Laudato Si'* and in favor of policies that harm the environment, fighting *against* a living wage and in favor of *laissez faire* capitalism (condemned since *Rerum Novarum* was written in the 1890s), fighting *against* a century's worth of magisterial calls for universal health care and denouncing the Church as "socialist" to shout down that call. None of that is "focusing on abortion" and none of it is prudential judgment. It is weaponizing the unborn in order to fight the rest of the Church's teaching by making the unborn the opposite of and competitor to all the human lives harmed and even killed by sins in these other areas.

## Issues Pertaining to the Body

The Church names such things as euthanasia, prostitution, artificial contraception and responsible procreation, sexual abuse, sexual promiscuity, and sterilization as prolife issues as well. Some of these are easier than others for many Catholics to grasp. Euthanasia is, fairly obviously to most people, the clear taking of innocent human life. But often people do not see a problem with many of the other things mentioned. This is due in part to the strong premium that post-moderns put on personal autonomy (a partially healthy reaction to the terrifying display of monstrous excesses of totalitarianism during the 20th century). Nonetheless, these issues remain signs of a profound loss of trust in God and in one another.

Scripture tells us, "Do you not know that your body is a temple of the Holy Spirit within you, which you have from God? You are not your own; you were bought with a price. So glorify God in your body" (1 Corinthians 6:19-20). A temple is a place of worship (that is, of love) and sacrifice.

The temple in Jerusalem offered animal and other sacrifices in prefiguration of Jesus' offering of his body and blood as a sacrifice in love for all of us. When Jesus drove out the moneychangers from the temple, he did so precisely because that temple was consecrated to love and sacrifice, not to commerce. When he said of his own body, "Destroy this temple and in three days I will raise it up" (John 2:19) he was likewise saying that his own body was offered freely and without reservation in love. And he was calling us to do the same. Therefore, anything that reduces the person to a mere commodity—whether it is slavery, prostitution, *in vitro* fertilization, or rent-a-womb technologies—turns people into things and elevates things like money above people.

Because the Church insists that our bodies, like Jesus' body, are gifts from the God who is Love and are intended for self-donating love, it therefore follows that the natural arena for that complete giving of self, when it is expressed sexually, is in marriage between one man and one woman (see Matthew 19:3-6). In the marital act, a man and a woman give themselves to each other completely and incarnationally by becoming "one flesh" (Genesis 2:24) and being fruitful (Genesis 1:28).

In other words, since God is the author of Nature, the Church urges that we keep sex natural and cooperate with, rather than technologically thwart his handiwork. The primary reason for the sexual nature of the body God has given us is loving union with the beloved and fruitfulness, much as the primary reason for eating is nourishment and the love and conviviality of the human community at table. Revelation says that God has not merely blessed our physical nature with the capacity for sex and the enjoyment of food but has elevated both sex and eating into sacramental encounters with himself in the sacraments of Matrimony and the Eucharist. Our animal natures are not the *opposite of*, but the *basis for*, our spiritual encounters with the God who has himself assumed an animal nature in Jesus Christ.

This is why the Church no more opposes the physical pleasures of sex than she opposes the physical pleasures of eating. But the Church also reminds us that first things come first and second things second. So she warns that using artificial contraception means elevating mere physical pleasure *above* love and fruitfulness in a way that puts second things first. It is something like elevating the mere taste of food over the greater goods of nutrition or the love of our neighbor. To place one's own pleasure—either with food or sex—above the love of neighbor and the fruitfulness of human love is to place oneself before other people, including one's spouse and children.

So the Tradition counsels trust in God and in one another. It calls for our generous response to one another and to new life in the faith that God will respond to such trust with even greater generosity and provision. For this reason, the Church does not object to family planning that cooperates with rather than thwarts the natural use of the body, just as she does not object to fasting from food but counsels against binging and purging. The idea is that our bodies are given to us to be offered as living sacrifices in love to God and to each other, not as raw materials to be manipulated at will without reference to the love of God or neighbor (see Romans 12:1-5). Grace and nature are a whole weave in the Catholic Tradition, and what we do with our own bodies very much affects our relationship with the God who gives us our bodies as well as the way we treat the bodies and souls of others.

Of course, the bitterest demonstration of how damage to one piece of the whole weave of Catholic teaching harms all is how sexual abuse by some clergy—and, far worse, bishops who have enabled that abuse—has harmed the credibility of the Church in teaching everything on the Dignity of the Human Person. Still and all, just as the sins of a math teacher do not falsify 2+2=4, so the sins of those entrusted with handing down the Tradition do not falsify the Tradition. Human life is sacred from conception to natural death, from Adam and Eve to the end of time. It is our part to defend the dignity of every human life, since Christ died for every human being.

## Questions:

1. What are some of the ways we can be tempted to elevate some classes of humans above others? How does the Tradition teach us to address such temptations?

2. What are some of the ways we can be tempted to demote some classes of humans below others? How does the Tradition teach us to address such temptations?

3. What does "prudential judgment" mean? Can you think of true and false applications of this idea?

# Chapter 3

# The Common Good:
# The Tradition of the Church

*I do not mean that others should be eased and you burdened, but that as a matter of equality your abundance at the present time should supply their want, so that their abundance may supply your want, that there may be equality. As it is written, "He who gathered much had nothing over, and he who gathered little had no lack."* - 2 Corinthians 8:13-15

Curiously, the Common Good—like Solidarity (which we will discuss in chapters 7 and 8)—is an aspect of Catholic Social Teaching that often affects the American ear in a profoundly different way than does the phrase "Dignity of the Human Person."

That is so because many fear that the Common Good is the Church's trendy nod to Marxism. In other words, they fear the concept of the Common Good is 1) a novelty (probably invented by Vatican II) and 2) something "liberals" in the Church pit *against* the Dignity of the Human Person as the Marxist pits the collective against the individual. But this is to misunderstand the very roots of the Church's teaching.

To begin with, the concept of the Common Good is not a trendy novelty. It is as old as—indeed, older than—the Church itself. It comes, in fact, from the Jewish tradition in the Old Testament and is, if anything, only ratified and universalized by the Catholic Tradition in the New Testament.

The primal saint in both the Jewish and Christian traditions is the man Paul calls "the father of us all": Abraham (Romans 4:16). Abraham is particularly remembered in Scripture for his fruitfulness and generosity rooted in faith. God makes him the father of many nations (the literal meaning of his name), and he shows constant generosity toward those around him.

Indeed, the mark of his call is that his life-giving generosity will ultimately touch the whole world to such a degree that God promises him, "In you shall all the nations be blessed" (Galatians 3:8). He is generous even to the wicked, famously dickering with God to spare the legendarily corrupt cities of Sodom and Gomorrah (see Genesis 18:22-32).

This brings us to one of the core biblical insights about the use of our gifts, whether spiritual or material. What is true for Abraham is intended to be true for all his spiritual heirs: namely, that *the Chosen are chosen for the sake of the unchosen.* Our gifts, whether in spiritual or material wealth, are given to us for the sake of those who do not have them—and those to whom much is given, much will be required (see Luke 12:48).

Accordingly, in the Old Testament, God commanded that Israel celebrate the Sabbatical and Jubilee years (Leviticus 25, 27), which required fields to lie fallow, debts to be canceled, and persons and goods to be released—indicating that everyone in Israel has a right to the common goods of the land God gave them. Private property, while real and good, was ultimately secondary to the good of the whole community, that is, the Common Good.

When Jesus, God made man, fulfils the law and the prophets, he embarks on his mission by applying the image of the Jubilee to himself and universalizing it to apply not to Israel alone, but to the whole world.

> And he came to Nazareth, where he had been brought up; and he went to the synagogue, as was his custom, on the sabbath day. And he stood up to read; and there was given to him the book of the prophet Isaiah. He opened the book and found the place where it was written,

> "The Spirit of the Lord is upon me,
>> because he has anointed me to preach good news to the poor.
>> He has sent me to proclaim release to the captives
>> and recovering of sight to the blind,
>> to set at liberty those who are oppressed,
>> to proclaim the acceptable year of the Lord."

> And he closed the book, and gave it back to the attendant, and sat down; and the eyes of all in the synagogue were fixed on him. And he began to say to them, "Today this Scripture has been fulfilled in your hearing." (Luke 4:18-19; Isaiah 61:1-2)

Jesus does not mean he is declaring a Jubilee year to begin his ministry. He means he *is* the Jubilee, just as he will later say he *is* the true Bread of Life prefigured by the manna in the wilderness (see John 6:35; Exodus 16) and he *is* the true temple prefigured by the stone building in Jerusalem (see John 2:19-21). What appeared only in sign and shadow in the Old Covenant is not revoked but revealed in fullness, in the Word made flesh. He does not come to abolish, but to fulfil the law and the prophets (see Matthew 5:17).

And so the Church insists that just as in the wilderness every Israelite had the right to eat the manna that God provided, so every person has the right to know the truth, mercy, and love revealed in Jesus Christ, the Bread of Life and the very embodiment of the Common Good. All our other efforts to promote the Common Good must keep that fact in mind.

But the Church does not spiritualize the law so as to deny earthly human needs. On the contrary, at the very dawn of the Christian revelation, John the Baptist will tell penitents asking what God requires of them: "He who has two coats, let him share with him who has none; and he who has food, let him do likewise" (Luke 3:11). In the same way, James says:

> What does it profit, my brethren, if a man says he has faith but has not works? Can his faith save him? If a brother or sister is poorly clothed and in lack of daily food, and one of you says to them, "Go in peace, be warmed and filled," without giving them the things needed for the

body, what does it profit? So faith by itself, if it has no works, is dead. (James 2:14-17)

And so the Catholic Tradition has long bound up the corporal or bodily works of mercy with the spiritual works of mercy and insisted that care for the human person means care for the Common Good of all, not just of people we happen to deem "worthy."

Someone may ask, "What about Paul's command that those who will not work shall not eat?" (see 2 Thessalonians 3:10).

To begin with, Paul is not speaking about the obligations of the *state*, but of Christians in the Church at Thessalonica who were ignoring their duties to the community on the theory that Jesus' return was imminent. He is speaking to those *within* the household of faith and telling them to get off their duffs—*so they can provide for themselves and for the Common Good.* He is not writing the First Epistle to the Americans on the Abolition of Welfare.

Meanwhile, the marching orders Jesus gives us as Christians moving in the world *outside* the household of faith are shocking and radical: "Give to him who begs from you, and do not refuse him who would borrow from you" (Matthew 5:42).

Note that he places absolutely no qualifications on this command. Indeed, what he says about generosity is wildly counter-cultural and counter-intuitive. He does not counsel giving only to "the deserving poor" who will thriftily earn a percentage on our largesse and pay us back with interest. Instead, he commands:

> When you give a dinner or a banquet, do not invite your friends or your brothers or your kinsmen or rich neighbors, lest they also invite you in return, and you be repaid. But when you give a feast, invite the poor, the maimed, the lame, the blind, and you will be blessed, *because they cannot repay you.* You will be repaid at the resurrection of the just." (Luke 14:12-14)

That's right. The one and only qualification Jesus offers for our charity to the poor is that we make certain the people we give to will *never* give us a return on our investment.

Why? Because it really is about the good of the other and not about us:

> For if you love those who love you, what reward have you? Do not even the tax collectors do the same? And if you salute only your brethren, what more are you doing than others? Do not even the Gentiles do the same? You, therefore, must be perfect, as your heavenly Father is perfect. (Matthew 5:46-48)

The gospel, as a quote often attributed to Dorothy Day says, "takes away our right forever, to discriminate between the deserving and the undeserving poor." Because in God's eyes we are none of us deserving, and we are all of us poor.

That is why St. John Chrysostom shocks us by saying that the rich exist for the sake of the poor, but the poor exist for the *salvation* of the rich.

St. John is not just making that up. He is paraphrasing the point of one of Jesus' most mysterious (to moderns) teachings: the Parable of the Dishonest Steward (Luke 16:1-13):

> "There was a rich man who had a steward, and charges were brought to him that this man was wasting his goods. And he called him and said to him, 'What is this that I hear about you? Turn in the account of your stewardship, for you can no longer be steward.' And the steward said to himself, 'What shall I do, since my master is taking the stewardship away from me? I am not strong enough to dig, and I am ashamed to beg. I have decided what to do, so that people may receive me into their houses when I am put out of the stewardship.' So, summoning his master's debtors one by one, he said to the first, 'How much do you owe my master?' He said, 'A hundred measures of oil.' And he said to him, 'Take your bill, and sit down quickly and write fifty.' Then he said to another, 'And how much do you owe?' He said, 'A hundred measures of wheat.' He said to him, 'Take your bill, and write eighty.' The master commended the dishonest steward for his prudence; for the sons of this world are wiser in their own generation than the sons of light. And I tell you, make friends for yourselves by means of unrighteous mammon, so that when it fails they may receive you into the eternal habitations."

In Jesus' day, a steward in charge of his master's finances made his living by adding a "service fee" on top of the money a debtor owed his master. So if you owed fifty measures of oil, the steward charged you for a hundred and kept the extra fifty. What the Dishonest Steward does is cut that fee off the top and simply charge the debtors what they owe his master so that they will be grateful to him and help him once he is booted from his job. In effect, he uses money to gain the gratitude of the poor debtors in the community.

Jesus' point is to turn the ancient idea of patronage—of currying favor with the rich—on its head. Far better, says Jesus, to curry favor with the poor since it is their prayers that will "receive you into the eternal habitations." For, "as you did it to one of the least of these my brethren, you did it to me" (Matthew 25:40). Use money as you use anything else, says Jesus: with a view to higher things than simply getting more money.

And so, just like the Church, Paul urges not the abolition of property, but its generous sharing modeled after that of Jesus, who "though he was rich, yet for your sake he became poor, so that by his poverty you might become rich" (2 Corinthians 8:9). Indeed, the model for what we are to do with our earthly riches is identical to the model we are to pursue with our spiritual riches:

> Having gifts that differ according to the grace given to us, let us use them: if prophecy, in proportion to our faith; if service, in our serving; he who teaches, in his teaching; he who exhorts, in his exhortation; he who contrib-

utes, in liberality; he who gives aid, with zeal; he who does acts of mercy, with cheerfulness. (Romans 12:6-8)

And the Tradition of the Church on this is unbroken from antiquity to the present:

St. Gregory the Great: "For if everyone receiving what is sufficient for his own necessity would leave what remains to the needy, there would be no rich or poor."[12]

St. Bede: "He then who wishes to be rich toward God, will not lay up treasures for himself, but distribute his possessions to the poor."[13]

Leo XIII: "Every person has by nature the right to possess property as his or her own. . . . But if the question be asked: How must one's possessions be used?, the Church replies without hesitation in the words of St. Thomas Aquinas: '*One should not consider one's material possessions as one's own, but as common to all*, so as to share them without hesitation when others are in need. . . .' True, no one is commanded to distribute to others that which is required for one's own needs and those of one's household; nor even to give away what is reasonably required to keep up becomingly one's condition in life. . . . *But when what necessity demands has been supplied and one's standing fairly provided for, it becomes a duty to give to the needy out of what remains over.*"[14]

---

12.   St. Thomas Aquinas, *Catena Aurea: St. Luke*, (Oxford and London: James Parker, 1874), 443.
13.   Aquinas, *Catena Aurea*, 445.
14.   Pope Leo XIII, *Rerum Novarum* 6, May 15, 1891. Available on-

Pius XI: "Yet when the State brings private ownership into harmony with the needs of the common good, it does not commit a hostile act against private owners but rather does them a friendly service; for it thereby effectively prevents the private possession of goods, which the Author of nature in His most wise providence ordained for the support of human life, from causing intolerable evils and thus rushing to its own destruction; it does not destroy private possessions, but safeguards them; and it does not weaken private property rights, but strengthens them.

"Furthermore, a person's superfluous income, that is, income which he does not need to sustain life fittingly and with dignity, is not left wholly to his own free determination. Rather the Sacred Scriptures and the Fathers of the Church constantly declare in the most explicit language that the rich are bound by a very grave precept to practice almsgiving, beneficence, and munificence."[15]

*Gaudium et Spes* 69: "God intended the earth with everything contained in it for the use of all human beings and peoples. Thus, under the leadership of justice and in the company of charity, created goods should be in abundance for all in like manner. Whatever the forms of property may be, as adapted to the legitimate institutions of peoples,

line at http://www.vatican.va/content/leo-xiii/en/encyclicals/documents/hf_l-xiii_enc_15051891_rerum-novarum.html as of December 11, 2019.

15.  Pope Pius XI, *Quadragesimo Anno* 49-50, May 15, 1931. Available on-line at http://www.vatican.va/content/pius-xi/en/encyclicals/documents/hf_p-xi_enc_19310515_quadragesimo-anno.html as of December 11, 2019.

according to diverse and changeable circumstances, attention must always be paid to this universal destination of earthly goods. In using them, therefore, man should regard the external things that he legitimately possesses not only as his own but also as common in the sense that they should be able to benefit not only him but also others. On the other hand, the right of having a share of earthly goods sufficient for oneself and one's family belongs to everyone. The Fathers and Doctors of the Church held this opinion, teaching that men are obliged to come to the relief of the poor and to do so not merely out of their superfluous goods. If one is in extreme necessity, he has the right to procure for himself what he needs out of the riches of others. Since there are so many people prostrate with hunger in the world, this sacred council urges all, both individuals and governments, to remember the aphorism of the Fathers, 'Feed the man dying of hunger, because if you have not fed him, you have killed him,' and really to share and employ their earthly goods, according to the ability of each, especially by supporting individuals or peoples with the aid by which they may be able to help and develop themselves."

Pope St. Paul VI: "[T]he right to private property is not absolute and unconditional. No one may appropriate surplus goods solely for his own private use when others lack the bare necessities of life. In short, 'as the Fathers of the Church and other eminent theologians tell us, the right of private property may never be exercised to the detriment of the common good.'"[16]

---

16.   Pope St. Paul VI, *Populorum Progressio* 23, May 26, 1967. Available

Pope St. John Paul II: "It will be necessary above all to abandon a mentality in which the poor — as individuals and as people — are considered a burden, as irksome intruders trying to consume what others have produced."[17]

So much for the idea that the Common Good is some sort of novelty in the Tradition.

But what about the perception that the Common Good is the opposite of and pitted against the concept of the Dignity of the Human Person? And what do we do about the Common Good if it is really part of the Church's Tradition?

## Questions:

1. What gifts has God given you and how do you give them away to others?

2. How are you poor and given riches by God? How are you rich and called to give to someone who is poor?

3. Can you think of a time somebody gave you something with no expectation of return? Can you think of a time you did that for somebody else?

---

on-line at http://w2.vatican.va/content/paul-vi/en/encyclicals/documents/hf_p-vi_enc_26031967_populorum.html as of December 11, 2019.

17. Pope St. John Paul II, *Centesimus Annus* 28, May 1, 1991. Available on-line at http://www.vatican.va/content/john-paul-ii/en/encyclicals/documents/hf_jp-ii_enc_01051991_centesimus-annus.html as of December 11, 2019.

# Chapter 4

# The Common Good: Basic Principles

*You are not making a gift of your possessions to poor persons. You are handing over to them what is theirs. For what has been given in common for the use of all, you have arrogated to yourself. The world is given to all, and not only to the rich.*
– St. Ambrose of Milan

Now that we know the Common Good is not a trendy novelty but comes from the very heart of the Catholic Tradition, we must next address the mistaken notion that the Common Good might oppose or contradict the Dignity of the Human Person.

The origin of this notion is fundamentally non-Catholic. It is the Calvinist idea of Total Depravity, the doctrine that the most fundamental fact about human beings is their sinfulness and therefore that the individual must always be at war with the rest of the human race.

To be sure, "all have sinned and fall short of the glory of God" (Romans 3:23). But that is not the most basic fact about us. On the contrary, the most basic fact is that we are made in the image and likeness of God. In other words, the Church starts with the Dignity, not the sinfulness, of the Human Person.

Note that: the Dignity of the Human *Person*, not the individual. To be a *person* is not the same thing as to be an individual. An individual is a sort of mathematical or political category. An individual exists as an atomized unit in isolation from and even in opposition to others. In contrast, Catholic anthropology understands that *persons* are fundamentally *in relationship with other persons*. Why? Because we are made in the image and likeness of God, who is *essentially* personal, existing from all eternity as a trinitarian *unity* and *relationship* of Father, Son, and Holy Spirit. These Persons live not in fear, oppression, or competition, but in perfect love, because God *is* Love (see 1 John 4:8). Therefore, we who are persons in his image are called to reflect that relationship. It is not good for man to be alone (see Genesis 2:18).

In Catholic teaching, exactly what disrupts relationships of love between persons and results in, among other things, oppression of the individual by the collective is sin. The idea that the Common Good is somehow pitted *against* the Dignity of the Human Person is a distortion grounded in fear; we fear that the collective will oppress the person.

In contrast, Catholic teaching does not see human beings as fundamentally at war with each other (though sin is certainly a reality), but as fundamentally in relationship with each other. Likewise, it does not see the four pillars of Catholic Social Teaching as pitted against each other, but as fundamentally in harmony. Catholic Social Teaching, unlike the three branches of the United States government, does not set its principles one against the other as "checks and balances" so as to maintain a "balance of power."

Fundamentally, Catholic Social Teaching is not about the use (or healing the abuse) of power, but about love. The right use—and healing the abuse—of power comes as a consequence of that.

Therefore, the Common Good is not the opposite, but the *extension*, of the Dignity of the Human Person. Because *each* person is made in the image and likeness of God, therefore *all* persons are. That means that we are to be *more* pro-life, not less. We are to make certain that *every* human being, not just the rich or the powerful, has the things God gifts to us. Since we are human *beings*, not human doings, our value lies not in what we produce, but in what we *are*.

## The Family: Icon of God and Building Block of Society

Since human beings are made in the image and likeness of a trinitarian God, the family—not the individual, state, or corporation—is a living icon of God and the basic building block of civilization. To a great extent, Catholic Social Teaching can be summed up in the principle: "If it's good for the family, it's good." The family is, indeed, described as the "domestic Church" (CCC 2203) and the first school of virtue and charity (CCC 1655). So the good of the family is profoundly important to the Common Good and the Church is the family's staunch defender, fighting for the sacrament of marriage, the sanctity of life, a living wage, "respect for and the integral promotion of the person and his fundamental rights, commitment to peace, the organization of the State's powers, a sound juridical system, the protection of the environment, and the provision of essential services [such as] food, housing, work, education and access to culture, transportation, basic health care, the freedom of communication and expression, and the protection of religious freedom" (*Compendium* 166). For all these things and many others are vital to the health of the family.

That said, it is vital to remember that building blocks are for *building*.

## The Family: Subordinate to the Kingdom of God

So Jesus says, shockingly, "If any one comes to me and does not hate his own father and mother and wife and children and brothers and sisters, yes, and even his own life, he cannot be my disciple" (Luke 14:26).

His point, of course, is not that we should wish evil on the family, but that nothing, not even the family, comes before our fidelity to the Kingdom of God, lest the family itself become an idol. Without the gospel, the human race is tempted toward the grave danger of falling into a sort of fertility cult in which things like blood, kinship, family, clan, race, and nation become not merely goods, but the highest goods. The gospel insists that, in the Kingdom, "There is neither Jew nor Greek, there is neither slave nor free, there is neither male nor female; for you are all one in Christ Jesus" (Galatians 3:28). Divorced from that Kingdom, mere exaltation of blood and tribe can become demonic ideologies of race—as American slavery and Jim Crow, American genocide of Native peoples, Australian genocide of Aboriginal peoples, Hutu genocide of Tutsi,

Turkish genocide of Armenians, and Nazi genocide of Jews have shown repeatedly.

But, of course, it's not just blood and tribe that can become idols. So can Mammon. And that idol is so dangerous that Jesus tells us plainly that we cannot serve it and God (see Matthew 6:24). We must choose. Unless we place our possessions at the disposal of the Kingdom they will surely possess us. Accordingly, the Tradition has always urged Christians to contribute generously to the Common Good and especially to keep in mind the "Preferential Option for the Poor."

## Justice and Charity

Anatole France once sarcastically denounced a legal system rigged to help only the powerful when he said, "The law, in its majestic equality, forbids the rich as well as the poor to sleep under bridges, to beg in the streets, and to steal bread." The idea of the Preferential Option for the Poor takes aim at exactly such false "equality." It is, like everything in Catholic teaching, rooted in Scripture. Deuteronomy 10:17-19 says:

> For the LORD your God is God of gods and Lord of lords, the great, the mighty, and the terrible God, who is not partial and takes no bribe. He executes justice for the fatherless and the widow, and loves the sojourner, giving him food and clothing. Love the sojourner therefore; for you were sojourners in the land of Egypt.

Note the paradox. God is "not partial." But how is this impartiality expressed? In the fact that he "takes no bribe" from the rich and that he "executes justice *for* the fatherless and the widow, and *loves* the sojourner." Through Isaiah, God commands us, "Cease to do evil,/learn to do good;/ seek justice,/correct oppression;/defend the fatherless,/ plead for the widow" (Isaiah 1:16-17).

This is a portrait of God as seen by the weakest, the outcast, the lowest, the poorest, and the most wretched. He takes their part and *prefers* them because while the rich have battalions of lawyers and tons of guns and lots of money, the weak and the poor have no one to defend them. We are called to do the same, particularly in light of the fact that when God became man he took his place with the least of these and literally had no place to lay his head (see Matthew 8:20). When he went on trial for his life against the will of the powerful, he too had nobody to defend him. It is the same now: what we do to the poor, we do to him (see Matthew 25:31-46).

At this point many get confused because they imagine that all help given to the poor is therefore "charity." So (the argument goes), it is fine for Christians to be personally generous to the poor. But what is the sense of involving the *state* in helping the poor? Aren't taxes just theft at gunpoint? And don't they simply mean that those who would have been able to freely give to the poor are now deprived of that opportunity by an overbearing state that *forces* them to be virtuous instead of letting them choose? Such arguments get repeated *ad infinitum*. But it is not Catholic teaching.

Why? Because it takes the focus off the least of these getting what they need and puts it on a power struggle over who gets the credit for helping them.

Here's the biblical truth: according to the Church, much of what we do for the least of these is *owed*, not charity. Failure to admit this is the colossal sin that the Rich Man committed in his neglect of Lazarus (see Luke 16:19-31). The Rich Man did not go to Hell for his failure to be *charitable*. He was damned because he refused to give Lazarus what he *owed* him.

Charity is *not* owed. Charity is charity. So if I am sitting next to you on the bus and don't hand you ten bucks I am not sinning against you because I do not *owe* you ten bucks. You have no claim in *justice* on my ten bucks. If I give you ten bucks that I do not owe you, that is charity: an act of loving generosity I need not have done but do anyway for love.

But if I step off the bus and find you lying on the sidewalk in a pool of your own blood and I do nothing, I deprive you of *justice* (not charity). Why? Because as a human being made in the image and likeness of God, you are *owed* your life and if I refuse to do what I can to help you, I risk the fires of Hell the Rich Man chose by ignoring Lazarus.

For exactly the same reason, the Good Samaritan did not show *charity* to the beaten man lying by the road (see Luke 10:29-37). Rather, he gave him what he *owed* him as his neighbor. By neglecting the wounded man the priest and Levite who ignored him sinned not against charity, but against justice, because the man had a *right* to live and they refused to pay him their just debt of help.

The Fathers of the Church saw this point plainly:

> St. John Chrysostom: "Not to enable the poor to share in our goods is to steal from them and deprive them of life. The goods we possess are not ours, but theirs."[18]

> St. Gregory the Great: "When we attend to the needs of those in want, we give them what is theirs, not ours. More than performing works of mercy, we are paying a debt of justice."[19]

> St. Basil: "Are you not then a robber, for counting as your own what you have received to distribute? It is the bread of the famished which you receive, the garment of the naked which you hoard in your chest, the shoe of the barefooted which rots in your possessions, the money of the penniless which you have buried in the earth. Why then do you injure so many to whom you might be a benefactor?" [20]

"Okay," you may say, "So it is justice and not charity to make sure that the needy get what they need. But why does the *state* have to be involved for me to do that? If I am *forced* to help by having my money confiscated in taxes

---

18.    St. John Chrysostom, *Hom. in Lazaro* 2,5:PG 48,992.
19.    St. Gregory the Great, *Regula Pastoralis.* 3,21:PL 77,87.
20.    Aquinas, *Catena Aurea: St. Luke*, 443-444.

to pay for universal health care, what good does that do my soul?"

The answer is that the state does not *need* to be involved if, in fact, the needs of the needy are being met. But as reality shows, quite often the needs of the needy are not met for a host of reasons. And that is why the state exists. Because it is the task of the state to ensure *justice*, not *charity:* to see to it that Lazarus does not starve, has drinkable water, has shelter, gets an education, has work, has functional roads, and gets adequate medical care. He is *owed* those things (and others) in justice because he is a human being and therefore has human rights. That is not socialist utopianism. That is bedrock Catholic doctrine about the Dignity of the Human Person and the demands of the Common Good.

> The responsibility for attaining the common good, besides falling to individual persons, *belongs also to the State,* since the common good is the reason that the political authority exists.... The individual person, the family or intermediate groups are not able to achieve their full development by themselves for living a truly human life. *Hence the necessity of political institutions, the purpose of which is to make available to persons the necessary material, cultural, moral and spiritual goods.* (*Compendium* 168 [emphasis mine])

There are two crucial things to note here. The first is that the Church puts the needy, not their benefactor, at the center of the Common Good. As of this writing, about one-third of all GoFundMe campaigns are devoted to people begging for somebody to help them pay for their enormous medical costs.[21] When parents of a girl with leukemia are facing astronomical medical bills, the issue is about caring for the child and saving her family from living under a freeway overpass, not the sanctification of their benefactor. If the state can provide health care for them without their economic destruction, then let it be provided. If some private benefactor can do it, then let him provide it. But the point, again, is providing for the health care needs of the sick, not who gets the credit for it.

And that leads to our second point: Because the Church puts the needs of the needy at the center rather than the method we use to meet those needs, she counsels us not to spend too much time worrying about questions like whether individual generosity or a state social safety net should be used to meet them. This is like worrying about which blade on the scissors does the cutting. In fact, developed nations with, for instance, a state health care system do not thereby render their citizens incapable of all personal charity. In the same way, developed societies are able to provide basic human necessities such as food and shelter both by private and public means for those who need them. Again, what matters is that those who have

---

21.  "GoFundMe CEO: One-Third of Site's Donations Are to Cover Medical Costs" by Gina Martinez, TIME, January 30, 2019. Available at https://time.com/5516037/gofundme-medical-bills-one-third-ceo/ as of June 14, 2020.

such needs find those needs met, not who gets the credit for meeting them.

## Universal Destination of Goods

God intends his provision to extend not just to an elite but to every human person. That is why it matters more that the needy have their needs met than that we get applause for it.

Catholic teaching, in fact, insists on the right to private property for all. The biblical tradition—specifically, the Seventh Commandment—teaches: "You shall not steal" (Exodus 20:15). Were there no such thing as private property, there could be no such thing as theft. So the *Compendium* (176) says:

> Private property is an essential element of an authentically social and democratic economic policy, and it is the guarantee of a correct social order. *The Church's social doctrine requires that ownership of goods be equally accessible to all*, so that all may become, at least in some measure, owners.

Yet the *Compendium* also tells us that, "The right to the common use of goods is the 'first principle of the whole ethical and social order' and 'the characteristic principle of Christian social doctrine'" (*Compendium* 172).

Many are confused when these passages are juxtaposed, taking the first as endorsement of private property and the second as endorsing some kind of Communism.

The truth is more profound. Just as the Common Good means that we are to be more affirming of the Dignity of the Human Person, not less, so it is more affirming of private property, not less.

Unrestrained Capitalism means (over time) the concentration of property in the hands of a few individuals. Communism means the concentration of property in the hands of the state.

The Universal Destination of Goods, in contrast, means that *everybody* should have a shot at owning private property. In other words, the Church opposes the unjust accumulation of property, whether in the hands of the state *or* in the hands of a few rich people. Private property is for all.

That is because things are made for man, not man for things. The goods of creation are given to all human beings, not just the strong. Just as we all have a right to be born, so we also all have a right to live.

At the same time, precisely because the Dignity of the Human Person means that things are made for human beings and not humans for things, even rights to property are subject to the right to life.

> *Christian tradition has never recognized the right to private property as absolute and untouchable*: "On the contrary, it has always understood this right within the broader context of the right common to all to use the goods of the whole of creation: the right to private property is subordinated to the right to common use, to the fact that goods are meant for everyone." (*Compendium* 177)

So, for instance, since water is essential to life, the system by which it is distributed to a community must be constructed in such a way that nobody is denied access to water because of an inability to pay for it. Systems that make water available at a profit are fine, just as long as those who cannot pay for this elementary and fundamental right are not cut off. In such cases, some other way of covering the cost must be found.

## Our Common Home

The mention of our common need for water brings us to the most recent development in Catholic Social Teaching: *Laudato Si'*. As we discussed in the beginning of this book, Scripture sees us as priest-kings and queens, set by God in the Garden of creation to till and keep that Garden. We are stewards of a trust given us by him, and the created world is invested with a sacred character because it is the work of God himself. Genesis teaches us not that God saw that it was neutral, but that God saw that it was *good*. Accordingly, creation is not there for us to use merely for our own benefit, but to cooperate with God in bringing forth its good fruits *for the good of all*. The same principle that applies to the universal right to water therefore applies to all the goods necessary to human life and flourishing.

Some fear that speaking of creation as "sacred" is to commit idolatry. But this not so. Creatures can have a sacred character without taking the place of God himself. So we speak, for instance, of the sacredness of human life without mistaking human beings for God. Indeed, to honor the sacredness of human life is to honor the Creator of human life. Likewise, respecting the work of God in creation is to respect nature's Creator. Conversely, to treat creation with contempt by pillaging, polluting, and poisoning it without thought for the Common Good is to prepare our souls to do exactly the same thing to human beings—and therefore to God. As Pope Francis says:

> Moreover, when our hearts are authentically open to universal communion, this sense of fraternity excludes nothing and no one. It follows that our indifference or cruelty towards fellow creatures of this world sooner or later affects the treatment we mete out to other human beings. We have only one heart, and the same wretchedness which leads us to mistreat an animal will not be long in showing itself in our relationships with other people.[22]

The reason for this is simple: human beings are made in the image and likeness of God and are the only creatures on earth whom God has willed for their own sake; nevertheless, they remain a part of nature. As St. Thomas Aquinas points out, grace perfects, not destroys, nature. Human beings are nature raised to personhood in God's image. That is why Scripture portrays the creation of man as God breathing life into "the dust of the ground" (Genesis 2:7). So what happens to nature affects us profoundly. If the water supply is poisoned, we die from drinking it. If

---

22. Pope Francis, *Laudato Si'* 92. Available on-line at http://www. vatican.va/content/francesco/en/encyclicals/documents/papa-francesco_20150524_enciclica-laudato-si.html as of May 8, 2020.

the food supply is destroyed by famine, we starve. If the air is poisoned by pollution, we suffocate. And if a new virus evolves and a pandemic breaks out, it can sicken and kill people around the globe.

Because of this, the gospel demands we face the fact that "There aren't two crises, one social and the other environmental, but two aspects of the same crisis."[23] Sin sends out ripples that harm more than the person next to us. Indeed, the ripples don't simply harm human beings. They can continue outward and harm the fabric of creation itself, poisoning the world, disrupting climate patterns and leading to horrific typhoons, unleashing devastating fires, creating patches of trash the size of France in the Pacific, and causing the extinction of whole species. So the gospel calls us not only to cooperate with God in the work of human redemption, but in renewing the face of the earth. And that too concerns the least of these because it is always the poor who suffer most from natural disasters. More than this, it concerns, yet again, the work of the state because global problems like pandemic and climate change (and the economic upheaval they cause) cannot be addressed by individual initiatives alone.

Does the Church then teach that a global welfare state should be established? Of course not. The poor are to have a share in the Common Good principally through work at a living wage, so that they might no longer be poor and might participate in Christ's work of salvation of the

---

23. Austen Ivereigh, *Wounded Shepherd: Pope Francis and His Struggle to Convert the Catholic Church* (New York: Macmillan, 2019), 200.

human race and the renewal of the face of the earth. And that brings us to the next pillar of Catholic Social Teaching: Subsidiarity.

## Questions:

1. Why is the Common Good not the opposite of the Dignity of the Human Person, but its extension?

2. What is the distinction between Charity and Justice? Can you give some examples of each in your life or in the lives of people you know?

3. What is meant by the Universal Destination of Goods? How does this fit in with the Church's teaching on the earth as our "common home"? Can you give some concrete examples of it from history or your experience?

# Chapter 5

# Subsidiarity:
# Being the Hands of God to Others

*We exhort you, brethren...to aspire to live quietly, to mind your own affairs, and to work with your hands, as we charged you; so that you may command the respect of outsiders, and be dependent on nobody.* – 1 Thessalonians 4:10-12

In the last two chapters we spent a good chunk of time on the role the state plays in serving the Common Good. This was necessary in much the same way that arranging the weight on a boat is necessary to keep it from capsizing. Our culture tends to be suspicious of the state and puts so much emphasis on the individual that mentions of the state's role in the Common Good are commonly met with fear and suspicion. Our goal in discussing the place of the state was not to cancel out individual responsibility for the Common Good but to briefly describe the state's legitimate role in helping to maintain it.

## The Basic Idea of Subsidiarity

Now we turn to our personal responsibility in maintaining the Common Good, and therefore to the third pillar of Catholic Social Teaching, the principle of Subsidiarity.

Subsidiarity means that, as far as possible, those closest to a particular need or problem should deal with that need or problem. The idea is that each person should have the opportunity to act *personally* as a sacrament of God's goodness and provision to the world and so be able to choose *personally* to cooperate actively with the grace of God in order to *be* that grace to others.

In Genesis, human beings take their place as unique cooperators with the work of God in creation: "The Lord God took the man and put him in the garden of Eden to till it and keep it" (Genesis 2:15). Scripture portrays creation not as a thing that happened once a long time ago, but as an unrolling act of God that continues throughout every square inch of the universe and every nanosecond of time right down to this moment. In the Psalms, God's creatures praise God simply by existing as the things God made them to be. But with human beings, new and unique dimensions are added: reason and choice. Humans praise God not only by virtue of being the kind of creature we are, but by choosing to praise him with our minds and bodies and by doing his will to do good to others. We willingly cooperate with him and not only offer him worship, but also love our neighbor. God gives us—as he gives no other creature—dominion over creation with the command to tend the Garden of creation, make the earth fruitful, and use our talents for the good of creation and the good of the community. Each one of us is therefore responsible to be fruitful with our abilities and resources for the Common Good. It is generally better that persons, each and every one, do their personal best to help in that than handing their responsibility off to somebody or something else (such as a remote bureaucracy). And, of course, the most basic way in which we do this is through the founding of or having membership in that first, tiniest, yet most important of societies—the family.

## A Common Misunderstanding of Subsidiarity

This seems straightforward enough, but in order to proceed with our discussion of Subsidiarity, we have to bring it into better focus, since this principle is often so misperceived that it appears almost like a photo negative of the true meaning of the Common Good.

What I mean is this: Just as many Catholics confuse the idea of the Common Good with socialism, so many 1) reduce Subsidiarity to Rugged Individualism and therefore 2) reduce much of Catholic Social Teaching simply and solely to that distorted definition. Not a few people imagine that Subsidiarity essentially means, "I should not have to pay taxes and the state should get out of my life." Likewise, I can't tell you how many times I have talked to Catholics who ring the changes on some version of, "Of course I believe in Catholic Social Teaching! I believe in Subsidiarity," as though the one is equal to and coterminous with the other.

In fact, Subsidiarity is not the opposite of the Common Good any more than the Common Good is the opposite of the Dignity of the Human Person. On the contrary, Subsidiarity builds on and harmonizes with both of these principles in the Church's thought. Catholic

Social Teaching cannot be reduced to Subsidiarity—and certainly not to Rugged Individualism. But neither can Catholic Social Teaching get along without Subsidiarity since Catholic Social Teaching is all about the reality that God wants every human being to be an active participant in bringing his love and provision to the world. So whenever possible, Catholic teaching insists that the people closest to a particular need or problem should be the ones to fill that need or solve that problem. That, in a nutshell, is Subsidiarity.

## Active Cooperation with, Not Passive Acceptance of, the Will of God

Subsidiarity harmonizes with the Dignity of the Human Person because in Christ's salvific work human beings are at the center, not as passive subjects but as active participants. As C.S. Lewis notes:

> He seems to do nothing of Himself which He can possibly delegate to His creatures. He commands us to do slowly and blunderingly what He could do perfectly and in the twinkling of an eye. He allows us to neglect what He would have us do, or to fail. Perhaps we do not fully realize the problem, so to call it, of enabling finite free wills to co-exist with Omnipotence. It seems to involve at every moment almost a sort of divine abdication. We are not mere recipients or spectators. We are either privileged to share in the game or compelled to collabo-

rate in the work, "to wield our little tridents." Is this amazing process simply Creation going on before our eyes? This is how (no light matter) God makes something—indeed, makes gods—out of nothing.[24]

Subsidiarity is crucial because every human being—made in the image and likeness of the Creator—is made for active participation in his creative work of saving a broken world. Our dignity in living out that reality makes our work a true participation in the work of God by assisting him in the creation and salvation of the world. We are "God's fellow workers" (1 Corinthians 3:9) because his work of creation and redemption is ongoing till the end of time.

Secondly, because each and every person has unique gifts to contribute to the Common Good, no person may be merged into the collective and lose his or her identity. We are immortals. The state (and any other system we create) is a temporary human artifact which exists only to stem the disastrous effects of the Fall. It exists for us, not we for it, because man is the only creature on earth God has willed for its own sake. And since we are material creatures who express our love and the grace of God through material means, each person should be able to own property so that each person has something to share with others.

Third, Subsidiarity is as essential as the Dignity of the Human Person and the Common Good because, more

---

24. C. S. Lewis, "The Efficacy of Prayer" in *The World's Last Night and Other Essays*, (New York: HarperOne, 2017), 8.

than merely sharing material things with others, we must share *our very selves* with others through our work. No small part of work is the joy of finding one's vocation or calling or mission in life—of discovering who we are and what God made and gifted us to be and do. We see it in the moment we realize we were born to sing or do science or heal others or teach or cook or do the myriad other things we love. To be sure, not every menial job is the fulfilment of our aspirations. But no small part of giving our life to others consists of discovering our gifts in doing work and realizing that we become more ourselves in the doing. It is the very opposite of being merged into a collective to find out who we are by discovering our gifts and talents. It is joy to discover our place in the community we love and serve and bless other people by bringing those gifts to the table.

And, of course, in the ultimate natural act of human fruitfulness and cooperation with God's creative will, we give of ourselves to one another in love so profoundly that we actually become participants in God's work of creating another immortal human person, a baby, and help to raise that human being to maturity through lives of deeply personal self-donating love and care.

## Mary as the Model of Subsidiarity

If you want to get the hang of it, think of the Blessed Virgin Mary as the icon of what we all do every time we say "Yes" to contributing to the Common Good. In the Annunciation, God comes to her personally. Mary does not receive a form letter addressed "To Whom It May Concern." God calls her by name as the human being she is. In the paradox of the divine plan, she has been prepared from all eternity with the graces and gifts she needs to do the work and bear the sufferings she must bear in accomplishing her mission. Yet at the same time she is given complete freedom to *choose* to say "Yes" or "No." And in her Yes Mary finds not slavery, but fulfillment. Her soul magnifies the Lord and her spirit rejoices in God her Savior (see Luke 1:46-47). Mary's "Let it be to me according to your word" (Luke 1:38) is not passive. It is a willed choice to actively cooperate with God's will. In that "Fiat!" she *chooses*, not merely acquiesces to bear the Word made flesh through her.

Every person who cooperates with the will of God is, to some degree or other, doing the same thing. Disciples of Jesus are conscious that they are cooperating with God because they are privy to his revelation that he is the vine and they are the branches and apart from him they can do nothing (see John 15:1-5). Others, like the sheep in the Parable of the Sheep and the Goats, may discover only later they were cooperating with God; at the time they thought that they were just "doing the decent thing." God, who does not care if he gets the credit, is not picky about that. What he cares about is our obedience to him because through it we are transformed into the likeness of his Son Jesus and our capacity to receive more grace from him increases and makes us happier.

This is why God gives us the gift of work.

## Tending the Garden

Some people think work is not a gift from God, but a curse. But this is not so. God places man in the Garden to "till and keep it." It is part of our primordial mission as creatures in the image and likeness of God to do fruitful work—part of the way in which we share in the creative work of God himself. Work has become more complicated and painful due to human sin and the curse it brings to all things we touch. Yet despite all that it has not ceased to be God's gift. Our dignity still dignifies our work.

Note that: we do not have dignity because we work. On the contrary, our work is dignified by the fact that we who are made in the image and likeness of God do it. We do not earn the right to exist by our work. Our existence is a free gift from God. But part of that gift is the right to work and, by that work, to receive the just reward of labor and to cooperate with God in providing his blessings to ourselves and others.

This, in fact, is the primary way in which most people contribute to the Common Good. Most children are housed, most naked people clothed, most students are taught, most bellies are filled, and most neighborhoods kept in good order by ordinary people going to work, caring for their families, and doing the ordinary things people do. God wills that we be his hands-on partners in shaping the world through our work and creativity. We provide goods and services, compose songs, invent medicines, create websites, fix cars, raise children, devise faster microchips, whip up new pizza recipes, create the wheel, write plays, and bust new dance moves as sub-creators acting in the image and likeness of the Creator.

## Just Reward for Labor

In return for a day's work, what we require (and what God demands that employers give their workers) is a living wage.

What is a living wage?

A living wage fulfills four criteria:

1. Families can live at a standard of decency appropriate to their society.

   The standard of decency changes and evolves over time, of course. Things that an average middle-class American thinks of as normal and ordinary, such as indoor plumbing or glass windows, would have been beyond the means of the wealthiest nobles of Richard Lionheart's court. Likewise, there are many places in the world where clean tap water is still a dream. But roughly speaking, of course, the idea is that people of average income should be able to live reasonably on the normal spectrum of their society.

2. They do so without working undue hours.

   The idea here is a balance between work, leisure, and sleep—about eight hours for each—with a day or two of rest for play and worship. Leisure, not forced labor, is the basis of culture. It is from leisure time that most of civilization has been born. Making time for play and hobbies and social pursuits and sports and goofing around is how civilizations stay healthy.

3. They do so without both spouses being forced to work outside the home (if they choose to do so, that's another story) or children forced to work inappropriate hours or under inappropriate conditions.

    The Church's social thought always puts a huge premium on the good of the family and on the chance for children to be children in a secure home close, if possible, to one or both parents.

4. They do so without undue reliance on government support or consumer credit.

    In other words, both employers and employees must practice fiscal responsibility. Employers must pay their employees enough that they are not forced to rely on welfare to make up what is insufficient in their pay. (So, for instance, corporate welfare in which taxpayers, not the employer, cover the insufficient wages of workers violates Subsidiarity). Likewise, workers must live within their means and learn to budget so that they can provide for their families, save for the future, and have enough to share with the community.

That is the goal. But in this fallen world, this goal (and many others in the world of human labor) is often not met.

Employers cheat. Workers goof off. Slipshod work is done, and so forth. What then? We will discuss that in Chapter 6.

## Questions:

1. How does Subsidiarity extend, not oppose, the Dignity of the Human Person and the Common Good?

2. What are some of the ways in which you are a source of God's provision and grace to other people in your life? How have people been that for you?

3. Where do you struggle to say to God, "Be it unto to me according to your word"?

## Chapter 6

# Subsidiarity:
# Going Up the Ladder a Rung at a Time

*If your brother sins against you, go and tell him
his fault, between you and him alone. If he listens
to you, you have gained your brother. But if he
does not listen, take one or two others along with
you, that every word may be confirmed by the
evidence of two or three witnesses. If he refuses to
listen to them, tell it to the Church.*
– Matthew 18:15-17

While Subsidiarity aims for the goal that each of
us should personally be about the business of loving our
neighbor, it also acknowledges that we live in a fallen
world where that often does not happen. So Subsidiarity
prudently teaches that when things are not working well
due to human sin and frailty, we should go up the ladder of authority carefully, one rung at a time, to deal with
problems. We see one illustration of that principle at work
in the words of Jesus above. But, of course, the same principle applies in many walks of life beyond conflicts in the
Church. Let's look at some other examples of Subsidiarity,
starting at the lowest rung: you and me.

## How Most Needs Get Handled

Here's a simple illustration. You need a loaf of bread. What do you do?

You don't phone the White House and demand the President send in the 101st Airborne to airlift you the bread. You don't call the mayor and demand the city provide you bread. You don't write a letter to the editor protesting the lack of bread in your pantry. In most cases, you go to the store and buy some bread. Or perhaps you like to bake, so you bake some. Problem solved. No Act of Congress required. You have, with your own skills and resources, seen to that need and exercised your human dignity to perform an act of love in the service of the Common Good and thereby grow in holiness. Tomorrow, your children will have toast for breakfast and go to school with a full belly and the promise of sandwiches in their lunchbags.

We live the vast majority of our lives by this commonsense rule. As G.K. Chesterton said:

> This is the first principle of democracy: that the essential things in men are the things they hold in common, not the things they hold separately. And the second principle is merely this: that the political instinct or desire is one of these things which they hold in common. Falling in love is more poetical than dropping into poetry. The democratic contention is that government (helping to rule the tribe) is a thing like falling in love, and not a thing like dropping into poetry. It is not something analogous

to playing the church organ, painting on vellum, discovering the North Pole (that insidious habit), looping the loop, being Astronomer Royal, and so on. For these things we do not wish a man to do at all unless he does them well. It is, on the contrary, a thing analogous to writing one's own love-letters or blowing one's own nose. These things we want a man to do for himself, even if he does them badly.[25]

Why? Because of the Dignity of the Human Person, that's why. It is best that we learn to provide for the Common Good ourselves for the same reason our children learn to do their own chores, be toilet trained, tie their own shoes, keep their own room clean, and bit by bit claim adult control of their lives so that they can live, love, work, play, worship, and be a gift to the world with their own time, talent, and treasure.

## Going Up the Ladder

Suppose, however, that a need is not getting filled by the person who would normally fill it. Suppose that for some reason you cannot get the loaf of bread. Here again we do not respond to the problem by racing to the top of the ladder of authority and requesting the President or the United Nations to intervene. We keep the center of activity

---

25. G.K. Chesterton, *Orthodoxy*. Available on-line at http://www.gutenberg.org/cache/epub/130/pg130-images.html as of February 3, 2020.

as close to home as possible. If, for instance, I am sick and cannot go get the bread, then some other member of the family can go instead. In that case, we have not even gone up the ladder one rung, because it is still a member of the family who is acting, and no outside help is needed to solve the problem.

Suppose, however, we cannot get bread because we have no money for bread and cannot fill the need with our own resources. At this point, the people capable of filling that need may be those nearest to our family. Maybe we are just temporarily pinched for money. So we ask our brother-in-law for a loan which we then promptly pay back on payday. Once again, problem solved.

Or maybe the need is more serious because we are out of work. Then we might approach one of the countless mediating institutions around us for help.

## Mediating Institutions

The term "mediating institutions" applies to a huge variety of human groupings unrelated to the state—everything from food banks to bowling leagues to theatre troupes to Facebook groups to the Boy Scouts to bird watching societies to cooking guilds—wherein human beings self-organize without the state or the Church telling everybody what do. The Church blesses this liberty and trusts that the Holy Spirit, in his immense fertility, will draw out from these ordinary human interactions a host of gifts and graces to the world from the charisms and human abilities the Spirit himself gives to us.

The Church says (*Compendium* 185):

> It is impossible to promote the dignity of the person without showing concern for the family, groups, associations, local territorial realities; in short, for that aggregate of economic, social, cultural, sports-oriented, recreational, professional and political expressions to which people spontaneously give life and which make it possible for them to achieve effective social growth.

In other words, the Church is not a vast centralized totalitarian system in which all is micromanaged by Rome and that which is not forbidden is compulsory. For the same reason, the Church desires that our secular order mirror this. Rather than the state running everything, a huge amount of the way in which we serve the Common Good goes through such mediating institutions.

As *Quadragesimo Anno* (79) puts it:

> Just as it is gravely wrong to take from individuals what they can accomplish by their own initiative and industry and give it to the community, so also it is an injustice and at the same time a grave evil and disturbance of right order to assign to a greater and higher association what lesser and subordinate organizations can do. For every social activity ought of its very nature to furnish help to the members of the body social, and never destroy and absorb them.

So when it comes to the loaf of bread we cannot afford, we might turn to our church or synagogue or food bank. We might set up a GoFundMe or put out a plea on Facebook for some help to tide us over till we get paid or find work. These are some of the many ways we can take a step up the ladder one rung to get the problem solved.

Sometimes, however, the problem is more intractable. For instance, we may face a situation where our need is chronic and more than small charities or local groups can help us to meet. So if we find ourselves, say, suffering from a debilitating illness, we might turn to the state for such things as food stamps and some form of income to help us get by—another step up the ladder.

But suppose now that there is another dimension to our difficulty in getting that loaf of bread. Suppose we go to the store to buy it and the store owner tells us he does not sell to people of our race or religion or something else. Now we are dealing with something which will require a different rung on the ladder—and possibly very many rungs if the local authorities cannot or will not help. So, for instance, the Civil Rights movement began when Rosa Parks was told she could not sit where she wanted on a bus. Local authority took the side of injustice. In response, unjust laws were challenged in court, then in higher courts, and eventually the highest authority of all passed the Civil Rights Act to dismantle an entire Jim Crow system of injustice.

Subsidiarity, then, "protects people from abuses by higher-level social authority and calls on these same authorities to help individuals and intermediate groups to fulfil their duties" (*Compendium* 187). Why? Again, because of the Dignity of the Human Person and the Common Good. The law is made for man, not man for the law. The person is not the means to a nice shiny functioning machine of government because the person is not a means to *any* end. Instead, the law had to change because Rosa Parks' dignity mattered more than The System.

Certainly, systems (of government, as well as plumbing, football rules, taxation, computer programming, and immigration law, to name a few) must exist. But they exist for the sake of the person, for each person, and therefore for all persons. Persons do not exist for the sake of systems and the moment a system becomes harmful to the human person it is right and proper to alter or, if necessary, abolish it and create a better one. And the system that allows each person to grow in genuine freedom and their full human dignity is best. So, as John Médaille points out, "Subsidiarity stands the idea of hierarchy on its head; instead of the lower serving the higher, higher levels of organization are justified only by providing an indispensable service to the lower, one that the lower could not provide for itself."

## The Church as a Model of Subsidiarity

Subsidiarity explains how the Church organizes herself too. On the one hand, the Church is universal. Indeed, that is what the word "Catholic" means. But the Church is also particular. So each diocese in the world is called the "particular Church" in that place. This expression of the Church is normatively ruled not by the Pope, but by the local bishop. The Pope does not micromanage the new paint job your parish needs. Indeed, even the local bishop doesn't do that, unless the parish organization is such a mess that your parish can't get it together and get the job done. Normally, the bishop would only step in if the local parish was bankrupting itself on the paint job. And normally, the Pope only steps into a diocese on the extremely rare occasion the bishop is letting things go to utter rack and ruin, a rack and ruin so disastrous that even the other bishops in that country cannot muster the wherewithal to help that diocese get out of its straits. Again, problems are handled by those close to the problem and only get bumped upstairs when those at lower levels of authority can't deal with it.

The instinct of the Catholic tradition, then, is always toward giving as much responsibility and power to the smallest rather than the mighty. Indeed, the mighty have power, in such a vision, precisely for the sake of the little. For the entire purpose of the greater power is not to acquire more power, but to ensure that the little and weak are able to participate to the extent they are able in the good of the earth, the work of human beings, and ultimately, in the life of the Blessed Trinity.

That's really what Subsidiarity is all about: participation. Therefore, the Church tends to favor systems that are democratic. This is nothing new, by the way. The oldest continuing democratic institution on the face of the earth is the Dominican order, which takes its decisions with the full participation of all its members. It was medieval Catholic Europe that, implementing the democratic forms created in the governance of monasteries, went on to invent both the *Magna Carta* (written by a Catholic cardinal) and the English Parliamentary system, not to mention the guilds in which common folk ordered their own affairs. The Church's habit is not to micromanage, but to leave people to figure out how to organize their own lives according to their best lights with confidence that the Holy Spirit will provide us with the wits and resources to do it ourselves.

That is why the Church does not hide its disapproval of

> *those countries ruled by totalitarian or dictatorial regimes* where the fundamental right to participate in public life is denied at its origin, since it is considered a threat to the State itself. In some countries where this right is only formally proclaimed while in reality it cannot be concretely exercised while, in still other countries the burgeoning bureaucracy *de facto* denies citizens the possibility of taking active part in social and political life. (*Compendium*, 191)

The Church wants people to have the freedom to work out their own affairs and exercise maximum creativity and love personally, rather than leave it to some bureaucracy or corporation to do it for us. Yet the Church also wants us to realize that those who are weak, poor, or wounded will need at times the help and protection of both the private sector and the state.

## Subsidiarity in a Global Context

The Church's resistance to totalitarianism should not be understood as resistance to international cooperation.

Again, the Church models what she seeks. Each diocese on the planet is the local expression of the Church governed by the local bishop; nonetheless the Church is a global unity in union with the Holy Father. Dioceses are not in competition with the global Church; we are all members of the one Body of Christ. And sometimes it is right and fitting for the Holy Father to act with global authority to coordinate the Church's efforts in council with the rest of the bishops for the good of whole Church.

In a related way, the Church insists that our common humanity as creatures made in the image of God means that there are—especially in a global economy and a world we now see more clearly than ever to be our common home—many issues which require a coordinated global response from the whole human race.

For example, global pandemic, by its very nature, requires a global response. Sharing information among the global health community, as well as sharing resources—from medical supplies to money to food and other necessities—is crucial and requires international coordination. Likewise, coordinated state responses overseeing public health measures such as "shelter at home" precautions (and the cooperation of an informed public) are critical to halting the rapid spread of highly infectious and deadly disease. In this way, Subsidiarity works at multiple levels. A family sheltering at home does its part locally. Higher up the ladder, health care workers do theirs in treating the sick. Still higher up, the scientific community works to coordinate data and research cures and vaccines. And that community, which is global, coordinates with state entities to make information and treatment available to all. Moreover, our globally-interconnected economy affects the fortunes of human beings all around the world and coordinated global efforts by state actors are necessary so that the sick receive care and the hungry are fed, not just in rich nations, but especially in poor ones.

Illustrations of the truth of this can be seen in the observance of Subsidiarity as well as in its breach. It was, for instance, a vast and well-coordinated global response that ended the threat of Ebola. Conversely, the lack of coordination in response to COVID-19 has contributed to high infection and death rates in nations that have failed to observe the public health requirements the disease imposes on us.

Or, to give another example, the urgent issue of climate change affects the entire planet and likewise requires a coordinated global response. This was one of the central points of Pope Francis' encyclical *Laudato Si'*, which followed the principle of Subsidiarity in urging us to act locally (by following commonsense rules for personal responsibility in not wasting the goods of creation, recycling, not overconsuming, reducing our carbon footprint, and so forth) while also thinking globally (by recognizing the fact this issue will require a global and supranational response). Pope Francis is not saying anything new here. He quotes his predecessor, Pope Benedict XVI, who himself cites previous Church teaching as he says:

> To manage the global economy; to revive economies hit by the crisis; to avoid any deterioration of the present crisis and the greater

imbalances that would result; to bring about integral and timely disarmament, food security and peace; to guarantee the protection of the environment and to regulate migration: for all this, there is urgent need of a true world political authority, as my predecessor Blessed John XXIII indicated some years ago.[26]

Note carefully: For Popes Francis, Benedict XVI and John XXIII, the idea of a "true world political authority" to address global issues is not a denial of Subsidiarity but yet another expression of it. It is the level of authority necessary to deal with problems at the global level just as an ecumenical council is the level of authority necessary to deal with global issues in the Church.

This is not, however, to say that there is no exception to the principle of Subsidiarity.

## Violence: The Exception to the Rule of Subsidiarity

I once had a friend named Rick, from New York City. Rick had a chum named Vinny. One day, as they were leaving work, Rick overheard Vinny talking to his roommate on the phone. As he hung up, Vinny said to his roomie, ". . . and don't forget to feed the burglar."

Intrigued, Rick asked what Vinny meant. Vinny explained that he and his roommate had come home and surprised a burglar in their apartment. Reasoning that the

---

26.  *Laudato Si'* 175.

City of New York would not punish him to their satisfaction, they decided to hold court in their apartment and mete out a punishment they felt was appropriate. So they found him guilty of burglary and sentenced him to thirty days in their closet. There he stayed with a mattress, a bucket, some books, and three squares a day for a month, at which point they let him go. They figured, "Who will believe him once we let him out?"

An intensely New York story to be sure. But here's the thing: the technical term for what Vinny and his buddy did is "kidnapping" and they would have rightly gone to prison for years had they been caught.

The reason is this: Subsidiarity holds true with one huge exception—the use of force and violence. In that case, the Church's teaching kicks things as far *up* the ladder of authority as it can. Vinny doesn't get to lock up burglars. Only the state gets to do that. Similarly, only the state is permitted to go around arresting, jailing, and (if necessary) killing people. Hatfields and McCoys are not allowed to inflict death penalties on each other. Lynch mobs are not allowed to hang people. Crips and Bloods are not allowed to execute each other.

Moreover, the bigger the act of violence, the more difficult the Church makes it even for the state to commit. If the police in Kobe, Japan are corrupt, the mayor of Seattle—Kobe's sister city—does not have the right to launch missiles in reprisal. If Japanese trade policies injure the state of Washington's economy, the governor cannot declare war on Japan. That authority gets kicked up the ladder to the federal government. And if governments actually listened to what Church has to say, the state would abolish capital punishment and war would get kicked up the ladder even further, to a supranational authority such as the United Nations.

The point is simply this: because inflicting violence ravages the Dignity of the Human Person and the Common Good, the Church seeks to make it as hard as possible. So the Church refuses to sanction its use by individuals except in very rare cases of justifiable self-defense. Meanwhile, at the top of the ladder of authority, the Church seeks to persuade governments to abolish capital punishment and to severely impede their power to wage war.

In short, the purpose of Subsidiarity is to make us saints who "take things into our own hands" as much as possible in the work of loving God and neighbor, not in the work of joining a vigilante mob. It is ordered toward helping us use our powers to love our neighbor to the fullest—and therefore to grow in Solidarity with all the other sons and daughters of Adam and Eve.

## Questions:

1. What is the basic reason for Subsidiarity as the Church understands it?

2. How does Subsidiarity normally work in everyday life? What happens if the people closest to a need or problem cannot meet the need or problem? Can you give examples from your own life?

3. What mediating institutions are you involved in that help meet the needs of the Common Good when individual efforts cannot? Can you think of one need in your community that is currently unmet and how you or that institution might help meet it?

# Chapter 7

# Solidarity: No Man is an Island

*No man is an Iland, intire of itselfe; every man*
*is a peece of the Continent, a part of the maine;*
*if a Clod bee washed away by the Sea, Europe*
*is the lesse, as well as if a Promontorie were, as*
*well as if a Manor of thy friends or of thine*
*owne were; any man's death diminishes me,*
*because I am involved in Mankinde;*
*And therefore never send to know for whom*
*the bell tolls; It tolls for thee.* – John Donne

The great Roman playwright Terence said, "I am a man. Nothing human is alien to me." It is significant that Terence was known for his comedies, since comedy is the art form that focuses most strongly on our weaknesses and our need for help from both divine and human grace and mercy.

In tragedies, the protagonists die isolated in their grandeur: great heroes left in splendid ruins while lesser beings look on in awe and say, "Now cracks a noble heart!" But in comedies, the quintessential ending has everybody come together at a great wedding banquet and all's well that ends well, not because they were geniuses, but because grace saved their bacon despite what fools these mortals be. It's rather like the Heaven that Jesus constantly compares to a wedding banquet: the Marriage Supper of the Lamb in which the poor, deaf, blind, and lame have the seats of honor. In comedy, we're all in this together and—being recipients of the Playwright's grace—we all get our richly undeserved rewards from the Founder of the Feast.

We're all in this together, nothing human is alien to us, and although life is a comedy, only a fool would say, "Hey buddy! Your end of the *Titanic* is sinking!" That is what Solidarity is all about. It is the idea that we are all debtors to gift givers both divine and human whom we can repay only by similar acts of generosity to one another.

## What is Solidarity?

Pope St. John Paul II tells us:

> [Solidarity] is not a feeling of vague compassion or shallow distress at the misfortunes of so many people, both near and far. On the contrary, it is a firm and persevering determination to commit oneself to the common good; that is to say, to the good of all and of each individual, because we are all really responsible for all."[27]

As with the Dignity of the Human Person, the Common Good, and Subsidiarity, Solidarity is rooted in Scripture. And, as ever, Solidarity does not contradict but

---

27. Pope St. John Paul II, *Sollicitudo Rei Socialis* 38, December 30, 1987. Available on-line at http://www.vatican.va/content/john-paul-ii/en/encyclicals/documents/hf_jp-ii_enc_30121987_sollicitudo-rei-socialis.html as of February 11, 2020.

harmonizes with the other principles of Catholic Social Teaching. So when Paul tells the Athenians, God "made from one every nation of men to live on all the face of the earth, having determined allotted periods and the boundaries of their habitation, that they should seek God, in the hope that they might feel after him and find him" (Acts 17:26–27), not only is he affirming a biblical teaching about the Dignity of the Human Person that dates back to Genesis 1, but he is also insisting that we all have a share in the Common Good God wills for us, and are all born to actively and personally participate in it. Solidarity emphasizes the *universality* and *interdependence* of God's provision for each member of the human race, as well as his call to us to play an active role in that provision.

## One in Adam

Christian faith begins, therefore, with a communal and familial understanding of the human race; because the human race springs from "one"—both the one God in whose image we are made, and the "one flesh" union of Adam and Eve, from whom the human race inherits its glorious yet fallen image.

The Faith insists that God begins with his natural creation and that his grace builds on this nature. Therefore, the Church's social teaching applies naturally not merely to Christians but to the whole human race since the whole human race is made in God's image and likeness. That is why the pagan Terence knew as well as the authors of Scripture the goods of human love, family, and a meal with friends—as well as the evils of murder, or a broken family, or theft.

This is why the Fourth through the Eighth Commandments don't tell Israel (or anybody else) something they didn't already know. Everybody has always known we are to honor our father and mother (and by extension our family, our neighbor, and our country). Everybody has always known that murder, adultery, stealing, and bearing false witness are wrong. Scripture itself makes this clear by telling us stories about Ham who insulted his father Noah (Genesis 9:20-27), Cain the murderer (Genesis 4:8-16), and the attempted adultery and vengeful act of false witness against Joseph by Potiphar's wife (Genesis 39)—all of which occurred centuries before the Ten Commandments were given to Moses.

So the point of this portion of the Ten Commandments is not to say that at Sinai God revealed these things to be sins, but rather to *ground* these universally known moral facts in God. Contempt for parents, murder, adultery, theft, and bearing false witness are bad *because they harm the creature made in God's image.* And since we are those creatures, sooner or later we have to acknowledge that we must do unto others as we would have them do unto us (see Matthew 7:12). We must forgive as we have been forgiven and we must be good to the stranger, the orphan, and the widow since we too can easily be in the same circumstances.

## Solidarity is Global

The Church notes that this natural law of generosity and interdependence is truer in the present period of history than ever. The *Compendium* (192) teaches:

> Never before has there been such a widespread awareness of the bond of interdependence between individuals and peoples, which is found at every level. The very rapid expansion in ways and means of communication "in real time," such as those offered by information technology, the extraordinary advances in computer technology, the increased volume of commerce and information exchange all bear witness to the fact that, for the first time since the beginning of human history, it is now possible—at least technically—to establish relationships between people who are separated by great distances and are unknown to each other.

The Church hails our increasing interconnectedness as a good thing. In our intensifying global culture, it is amazing and wonderful that I can and do have friends not only all over the U.S., but in the UK, Australia, China, Singapore, Hong Kong, New Zealand, France, Canada, Portugal, Italy, Germany, Nigeria, the Gambia, and Uganda. Technology has shrunk the world and brought close to us people who only a few years ago were in unthinkably faraway places with strange-sounding names. Now it is commonplace to be consciously aware of the lives, needs, and hearts of people all over the globe in ever-expanding circles of friends and family. I can receive a request for help from my Gambian friend, post it on Facebook, and within seconds people from Wichita to Glasgow to Sydney are part of a network of prayer or financial support that sustains his life. But, of course, original sin extends to our global culture as well. So the *Compendium* (192) continues:

> *In the presence of the phenomenon of interdependence and its constant expansion, however, there persist in every part of the world stark inequalities between developed and developing countries,* inequalities stoked also by various forms of exploitation, oppression and corruption that have a negative influence on the internal and international life of many States. *The acceleration of interdependence between persons and peoples needs to be accompanied by equally intense efforts on the ethical-social plane,* in order to avoid the dangerous consequences of perpetrating injustice on a global scale. This would have very negative repercussions even in the very countries that are presently more advantaged.

In short, our global culture doesn't just make it easy for me to pray for my Nigerian friend, it makes it easy for others to prey on him. Because of original sin, it also makes it easy to exploit or even enslave his child for a morning cup of cocoa.[28] We are caught up in the life-and-death

---

28. "2.3 million children work in the cocoa fields of Ghana and Côte d'Ivoire. These children are vulnerable to brutal labor practices, including trafficking and slavery. Candy companies—including

struggle between our God-given interdependence and our fallen and increasingly radical inequalities, and the Church calls us to work so that everybody in the human family has a just share in the goods of the earth God has given us.

We can start doing this work by seeing the relationship between rich and poor as the gospel does. We are all in this together, insists the gospel. Paul tells the Romans that the baptized are "members" (that is, body parts) not only of Christ, but of one another (see Romans 12:5). And, of course, as we have seen, any person we meet is our neighbor and therefore is Jesus Christ in disguise (see Luke 10:29-37; Matthew 25:31-46). Moreover, the Christian tradition warns that the rich, not the poor, are in far greater danger and in far greater need if they do not share with the poor.

As G.K. Chesterton says:

> Only the Christian Church can offer any rational objection to a complete confidence in the rich. For she has maintained from the beginning that the danger was not in man's environment, but in man. Further, she has maintained that if we come to talk of a dangerous environment, the most dangerous environment of all is the commodious environment. I know that the most modern manufacture has been really

---

but not limited to Nestlé, Hershey, Cargill, ADM, and Barry Callebout—have admitted accountability and promised to remedy this situation. Sadly, 17 years has passed since this agreement and little has changed." See http://www.slavefreechocolate.org/ for more information.

occupied in trying to produce an abnormally large needle. I know that the most recent biologists have been chiefly anxious to discover a very small camel. But if we diminish the camel to his smallest, or open the eye of the needle to its largest—if, in short, we assume the words of Christ to have meant the very least that they could mean, His words must at the very least mean this—that rich men are not very likely to be morally trustworthy. Christianity even when watered down is hot enough to boil all modern society to rags. The mere minimum of the Church would be a deadly ultimatum to the world. For the whole modern world is absolutely based on the assumption, not that the rich are necessary (which is tenable), but that the rich are trustworthy, which (for a Christian) is not tenable. You will hear everlastingly, in all discussions about newspapers, companies, aristocracies, or party politics, this argument that the rich man cannot be bribed. The fact is, of course, that the rich man is bribed; he has been bribed already. That is why he is a rich man. The whole case for Christianity is that a man who is dependent upon the luxuries of this life is a corrupt man, spiritually corrupt, politically corrupt, financially corrupt. There is one thing that Christ and all the Christian saints have said with a sort of savage monotony. They have said simply that to be rich is to be in peculiar danger of moral wreck. It is not demonstrably un-Christian to kill the rich as violators of definable justice. It is not demonstrably un-Christian to crown the rich as convenient rulers of society. It is not certainly un-Christian to rebel against the rich or to submit to the rich. But it is quite certainly un-Christian to trust the rich, to regard the rich as more morally safe than the poor.[29]

In the Old Testament, the warnings to the rich and powerful are stark:

You shall not wrong a stranger or oppress him, for you were strangers in the land of Egypt. You shall not afflict any widow or orphan. If you do afflict them, and they cry out to me, I will surely hear their cry; and my wrath will burn, and I will kill you with the sword, and your wives shall become widows and your children fatherless. (Exodus 22:21-24)

Note that in Old Testament passages like this, the horizon of consequences for our actions extends only to this life. If Israel harms the poor, God warns them of earthly consequences. If Israel cares for the poor, God promises Israel earthly blessings such as prosperity or long life.

But with the coming of Jesus Christ, though the same moral principles remain intact, the horizon of consequences

---

29. G.K. Chesterton, *Orthodoxy*. Available on-line at https://www. gutenberg.org/files/16769/16769-h/16769-h.htm as of February 12, 2020.

is now revealed to extend to *eternity*. The gospel ups the ante and reveals that not merely earthly blessing or suffering awaits us, but everlasting ecstasy or everlasting loss.

> [A]nd he will place the sheep at his right hand, but the goats at the left. Then the King will say to those at his right hand, "Come, O blessed of my Father, inherit the kingdom prepared for you from the foundation of the world ... Then he will say to those at his left hand, 'Depart from me, you cursed, into the eternal fire prepared for the devil and his angels ... And they will go away into eternal punishment, but the righteous into eternal life." (Matthew 25:33-34, 41, 46)

Remember St. John Chrysostom: The rich exist for the sake of the poor, but the poor exist for the *salvation* of the rich. The poor are in desperate need of the help of the rich, but the rich are in even more desperate need of the prayers of the poor. They stand in eternal peril if the poor curse their names before the Throne of Almighty God for harming them. So just as Jesus urges the rich to use their wealth for blessing the poor that they may be welcomed into "eternal habitations" (Luke 16:9), likewise Revelation warns us not to earn the terrible curses of the poor who cry out, "O Sovereign Lord, holy and true, how long before you will judge and avenge our blood on those who dwell upon the earth?" (Revelation 6:10). When the poor offer prayers of gratitude for (or anguished cries for justice against) the rich, that may spell the difference between Heaven and Hell for the rich. For inasmuch as we do it for (or to) the least of these, we do it for (or to) Jesus himself.

The Church tells us that Solidarity is both "a *social principle* and ... a *moral virtue*" (*Compendium* 193). In other words, it is a natural dimension of how humans are supposed to live; but—since we are fallen and often behave at odds with our own best interests—it is also a virtue we have to intentionally cultivate by denying ourselves, taking up our cross, and following Jesus.

Disciples of Jesus are conscious of the need for such virtue because they listen to the gospel. But non-Christians too can—and often do—grasp this need for self-denying generosity. Anybody can choose to put others before themselves. It is something that parents, patriots, and decent people have done everywhere and all through history. And every person who attempts it will tell you the same thing: it is difficult. Moral virtues are won on the battlefield of human choice.

Obvious case in point: the duty of generosity. Generosity sounds good on paper. All of us together are stronger, happier, and healthier than each of us alone and relying only on our own meager resources to get by in life. But, in practice, generosity means refusing my natural inclination to clutch my stuff and risking to share it with somebody who might cheat me, or do something I disagree with, or not share with me when I am in need. To this instinct the biblical tradition says, "Yes, it's scary. Be generous anyway" and commends, again and again, the righteous person in these terms:

> One man gives freely, yet grows all the richer;
> another withholds what he should give,
> and only suffers want. A liberal man will be

enriched, and one who waters will himself be watered. (Proverbs 11:24-25)

And, as the story of the Widow's Mite (Mark 12:41-44) makes clear, generosity is determined according to one's means, not according to a specific dollar amount. The Widow had but a couple of pennies to offer, but nonetheless she gave generously of what little she had—as is often the case with the poor.

Relatedly, the question "Who is the poor person I should care for?" is much the same as "Who is my neighbor?": anyone whose need you can help fill in the way most appropriate to their dignity.

But what if you cannot fill their need? Suppose you only have two copper coins, like the Widow? Subsidiarity bids us do what we can, and then go up the ladder one rung to see if somebody else nearby can help supply the need. So the Good Samaritan does what he can for the beaten man. But then he gives that man to the care of an innkeeper who has resources he himself lacks. In the case of the Samaritan, he promises to repay the innkeeper. In other cases, when such a promise may be impossible, other arrangements must be made.

In our own time, we might need to turn to other people, institutions, or the state to supply what we cannot. All of these alternatives rest on one bedrock idea: that our Solidarity with one another means that the community must do what it can to help those in need since each is responsible for all and all are responsible for each.

## What We Owe Each Other

Some think that we can live in a stateless society of pure individualism. But this simply is not so. By our very nature, we are born into a world where it is our glad burden to owe debts to God and to our fellow human beings that we can never repay. We owe God an unpayable debt for literally everything. But we also owe our family, our country, our civilization, and the entire human race for a colossal bounty of gifts. They gave us food, clothing, shelter, education, language, Shakespeare, fishing, physics, a million recipes, *Star Wars*, the Beatles, Homer, the Bible, bubble gum, pencils, penicillin, aspirin, automobiles, indoor plumbing, and a billion other things we could never have thought of, much less created on our own. We depend on others—and on the organizing power of the state—for a host of things. Therefore, we owe those people—and the state—a debt not of charity but of justice, to help advance the work we do in common for the good of all. That is why Scripture describes taxes, not as "theft" but as something we do, in fact, *owe* (see Romans 13:7). Why?

Because our freeway system was not built and is not maintained by small bands of local citizens patching potholes on Saturday afternoon. The state does that.

Because an educated population of millions did not just happen. They went through school systems that were largely the creation of the state.

Because when a despot like Hitler declared war, he was not met by some volunteers who grabbed their pistols and headed across the Atlantic in a dinghy to land at Normandy. The state made it possible to defeat Nazi Germany.

Because when Ebola was raging, the cure was not found by one plucky guy with his chemistry set, but by a vast coordinated effort of states and private actors.

Of course, being human creations, no state system is flawless. Nevertheless, St. Paul understood the state to be so vital in forming a more perfect union, establishing justice, ensuring domestic tranquility, providing for the common defense, promoting the general welfare, and securing the blessings of liberty to ourselves and our posterity—that is, to maintaining the Common Good—that he told the Church that state authorities "are ministers of God" (Romans 13:6).

The Church understands (none better) that this does not mean the state is holy, infallible, or unquestionable. It is the state, after all, that murdered the Son of God. So when the state tried to order the apostles to stop preaching the gospel, the apostles replied "We must obey God rather than men" (Acts 5:29). And four centuries later, Augustine summarized why that is so: because an unjust law is no law at all. But even a deeply unjust state can still have legitimate laws we must obey. Murderers were rightly jailed even in Stalin's despotic USSR. Armed robbery was legitimately punishable even if you lived in the tyrannical Third Reich. And Paul tells the Romans to obey Caesar even though the Caesar of whom he wrote was Nero, the psychopath who would eventually cut off his head.

Which means that Solidarity has a dark side we have to discuss in our next chapter.

## Questions:

1. Define Solidarity and give some examples of what it looks like in the real world.

2. Can you think of ways in which we live in debt to God and our community? Can you think of ways in which you can pay that debt forward to your neighbor?

3. What are some of the challenges you face in living out the principle of Solidarity on a practical basis?

# Chapter 8

# Solidarity:
# Struggling Together in Sin and Hope

*Generations have trod, have trod, have trod;*
*And all is seared with trade; bleared, smeared*
*with toil;*
*And wears man's smudge and shares man's*
*smell: the soil*
*Is bare now, nor can foot feel, being shod.*

*And for all this, nature is never spent;*
*There lives the dearest freshness deep down*
*things.* – Gerard Manley Hopkins

## Structures of Sin

The mention of the "dark side" of Solidarity brings us to another idea that we must touch on: Structures of Sin. The *Compendium* (119) describes them this way:

> *These are rooted in personal sin and, therefore, are always connected to concrete acts of the individuals who commit them, consolidate them and make it difficult to remove them.* It is thus that they grow stronger, spread and become sources of other sins, conditioning human conduct. These are obstacles and conditioning that go well beyond

the actions and brief life span of the individual and interfere also in the process of the development of peoples, the delay and slow pace of which must be judged in this light. The actions and attitudes opposed to the will of God and the good of neighbour, as well as the structures arising from such behaviour, appear to fall into two categories today: "on the one hand, the all-consuming desire for profit, and on the other, the thirst for power, with the intention of imposing one's will upon others. In order to characterize better each of these attitudes, one can add the expression: 'at any price.'"

In short, sin begins in the heart, but it does not stay there. It gets expressed in what we do. So the things we make reflect, among other things, the sins that live in our hearts. This isn't true merely of artists who make pornography or manufacturers who make shoddy products. It suffuses everything we make, and especially the gigantic, globe-spanning political, social, and economic systems we create to dominate the world.

## A Biblical Example of a Structure of Sin

To give an example of what is meant by a Structure of Sin, see Acts 19:23-41. When Paul went to Ephesus to preach the gospel he did not simply threaten a religious system that worshipped Diana, the Moon Goddess. He threatened an entire socio-economic and political system organized around her temple, one of the Seven Wonders of the World.

119

Consequently, it was not just a gaggle of random members of the cult of Diana that attacked him. It was a mob organized and spurred on by the silversmiths of Ephesus, who made their living selling Diana trinkets to pilgrims. The gospel threatened (and in good time would eventually dismantle) a religio-economic-socio-political Structure of Sin in Ephesus that stood opposed to the Kingdom of God.

Now we—to the degree we all sin—are all idolaters just like the Ephesians, since sin is the disordered attempt to get our deepest happiness from something other than God. Our Big Four in the pantheon of idols are (and always have been) Money, Pleasure, Power and Honor. And, just as the Ephesian silversmiths did, we too create political and economic systems to support our idols.

This results in the creation of idolatrous political and economic systems that fight against those trapped within them, especially against those who are genuinely trying to do the right thing—just as the political and economic structures in Ephesus fought against Paul. So, for instance, we see just such a conflict in the early United States when the Founding Fathers who fought (sincerely enough) for the proposition "all men are created equal" nonetheless were trapped in the Structure of Sin known as a "slave economy" and could not find a way to get rid of it. Result: Thomas Jefferson, the man who wrote the *Declaration of Independence* and said of slavery, "Indeed, I tremble for my country when I reflect that God is just: that his justice cannot sleep forever,"[30] never freed his own slaves.

---

30. Thomas Jefferson, *Notes on the State of Virginia, Query*

The system of slavery helped enslave Jefferson to what his own conscience told him was the grave sin of owning slaves. This does not absolve Jefferson of his sin. After all, others of his time *did* free their slaves. But it remains the case that Structures of Sin can both blind and bind us from seeing and acting on evil that later generations (and sometimes even we ourselves) rightly regard with repugnance. They exert enormous pressure on people to acquiesce to sin while providing them with countless excuses, often against the cries of their own conscience, to do so.

Similar situations apply today concerning a host of human institutions. A person who works, for example, for a corporation where an increase in profits is the only measure of success, will be pressured and even compelled by fear of losing his job to act in certain ways that may not be in accord with the gospel. Institutions provide structures that guide decision-making and set up systems of rewards and sanctions. The question is whether these systems reward the good or do the opposite. That is why the Tradition insists that, in addition to confronting our personal sins, Structures of Sin must be battled as well, since they exert pressure on us to not repent our personal sins—and they often blind us from even seeing that the Structure of Sin exists. This is a dynamic that applies in all institutions and must be confronted in all institutions--even the Church, as the clerical sexual abuse scandal abundantly illustrates.

---

*XVIII: Manners*, 1781. Available on-line at https://teachingamericanhistory.org/library/document/notes-on-the-state-of-virginia-query-xviii-manners/ as of July 3, 2020.

## The Gospel Calls Us to Challenge Structures of Sin

The gospel has done this many times in history from ending murderous games in the Roman Colosseum, to the abolition of slavery, to reforming unjust labor laws, to enacting the Civil Rights Act. Such a process nearly always occurs with agonizing slowness, since it takes human beings centuries to grope toward pulling down such structures, especially given that huge amounts of money, power, and the sheer dead weight of human habit oppose such change. Still, dismantling Structures of Sin can be done and the leaven of the gospel has repeatedly been kneaded into societies in order to do it.

When that has happened, the gospel has usually changed these Structures of Sin by means of a combination of moral suasion and the help of the state. So, for instance, the barbaric Games in Rome ended when Christian monks confronted the cheering mobs with their own consciences by entering the arena—where for centuries people had been forced to kill each other or be mauled by wild beasts— shouting, "For God's sake, forebear!" The brutality was outlawed by the increasingly Christianized state because citizens' consciences could no longer endure it. For the same reason, crucifixion was banished by that same state because it could no longer bear to inflict on other human beings what it had once inflicted on the Son of God.

In the 19th century, the great English Evangelical William Wilberforce likewise made the slave trade morally unbearable to the English conscience and, with the help of the state, abolished it. In the United States, Christian abolitionists likewise made slavery intolerable to the consciences of many Americans before the state abolished it by force of law. A century later, the Civil Rights movement continued the unfinished work of the Civil War abolitionists through the moral appeal of people like Dr. Martin Luther King, Jr. who again worked against the Structure of Sin called "Jim Crow" both via citizen protests and with the state to pass the Civil Rights Act.

Again, this does not mean the state itself cannot be a Structure of Sin. It obviously can. But it is also the case that the state can be an instrument for healing Structures of Sin—and that on many occasions such healing would have been impossible without the help of the state since it alone has sufficient power to back reform with the force of law.

So, for instance, take the examples of abusive priests and brutal police. Instead of either denying the problem or issuing a blanket condemnation of priests and police, the wise approach is to face the fact that predators go where prey is, whether on the African savannah or in human institutions. Those predators attracted to violence will seek out professions where it is permitted, such as police, security, and the military—because that is where the prey they seek are to be found. Likewise, sexual predators will naturally gravitate to institutions that put them in contact with the prey they seek, whether in schools, day cares—or the priesthood. Institutions seeking candidates to fill those necessary roles must confront that fact and create mechanisms for both screening such predators from entry and (since no such mechanism is perfect) for expelling and punishing them when they manifest.

It is crucial to understand that all institutions, like all machines, do not do what we *want* them to do: they do what we *design* them to do. If we design institutions to do this work of screening and removing predators, we will have far fewer predators. If we do nothing, we invite into those institutions predators who will turn those institutions into machines that will protect and even create more predators.

The point is this: Structures of Sin make it hard to be good and often punish us for trying while blinding us from even being able to see the good. Healthy institutions, in contrast, make it much easier to do the right thing and even reward us for trying. Structures of Sin are usually reformed—or, where necessary, dismantled—through good actions by each person, together with good statecraft and just laws so that, by the grace of God, his Kingdom can come and his will be done on earth as it is in Heaven.

## Reforming Structures of Sin Involves Both Personal and Communal Effort

The *Compendium* (193) is clear about what is required to change Structures of Sin:

> They must be purified and transformed into *structures of solidarity* through the creation or *appropriate modification of laws, market regulations, and juridical systems* [emphasis mine].

In short, non-state efforts to effect change (e.g., boycotts of corporations who support abortion or use child slaves, or mass marches against police brutality) are wonderful, but very often it is necessary to change legal, political, social and economic structures by the force of law as well. Here, not just the citizen but the state bears a responsibility.

This does not relieve individuals of responsibility for Solidarity or the Common Good. Indeed, attempts to effect change merely by force of law without winning the consciences of most of the citizenry can often be doomed, as Prohibition demonstrated. Therefore, since the state neither can nor should do a great deal of moral formation, the responsibility falls squarely on our shoulders as good citizens, husbands, wives, sons, daughters, workers, employers to make it our personal and hands-on business to love our neighbors by teaching them. This is particularly true under a system of government where citizens elect representatives who create the laws. After rendering his taxes unto Caesar, Jesus (who was so poor he had nowhere to lay his head) still found plenty of opportunities to go about doing good. We should do the same.

For Christians, this unbreakable bond between our private thoughts and our public acts is what St. James is getting at when he says, "[F]aith by itself, if it has no works, is dead" (James 2:17).

## Paying Our Debt Forward

The Church's insistence on Solidarity is often deeply threatening to much of Western — especially US American — culture. Many have internalized the belief that the law should concern itself principally with "my wants" and think the chief criterion of the good is "consent." We often approach both God and neighbor without understanding something that was obvious to our ancestors and is the very heart and soul of Solidarity: namely, that we live in a permanent relationship of *debt* to God, to all who come before us, and to all who come after us. According to the Church, we stand in that relationship of debt more than we can even imagine, much less repay. In the words of the *Compendium* (195):

> *The principle of solidarity requires that men and women of our day cultivate a greater awareness that they are debtors of the society of which they have become part.* They are debtors because of those conditions that make human existence livable, and because of the indivisible and indispensable legacy constituted by culture, scientific and technical knowledge, material and immaterial goods and by all that the human condition has produced.

We owe our existence—and the existence of all that is—to God. But we also owe a debt to all who came before us and to the vast interconnecting web of relationships that sustains us at this very hour. Without the civilization they built—without Mozart, the Epic of Gilgamesh, the utility that is making sure your electricity is on right now, the creators of the trucking network who made sure you got the meat for your sandwich at lunch, your Mom who taught you to tie your shoes, the Framers of the Constitution, the scribes who invented the alphabet, the people monitoring weather satellites, the nuns and priests who invented hospitals, the martyrs who died for Christ, the people who cooked up the scientific method, Augustine, Thomas

Aquinas, Hildegard of Bingen, Maimonides, Les Paul, Ed Sullivan, Gregor Mendel, the guy who made the first shoe, invented the wheel, invented the zero, discovered fire, and thought of agriculture—you and I would be bawling naked beasts in a howling wilderness or in all likelihood would have died in our infancy.

But we don't just owe a debt to those who came before us. We owe a debt to pay it forward to our children just as our ancestors have paid it forward to us. We owe this debt because Jesus has commanded us to love one another as he has loved us.

That is *how* our debt to him is repaid: by paying it forward to our neighbor we love the God who needs nothing from us and to whom we can give nothing that is not already his. Similarly, when we refuse to give generously (and this includes, especially, the forgiveness of enemies), we stand at risk of facing the same judgment as the servant in the parable who, having been forgiven a debt of millions by the King, turns on a fellow servant who owes him a paltry sum and treats him mercilessly. When the King discovers his treatment of his fellow servant and his refusal to "pay forward" the mercy that he received, the King condemns him not for his debt, but for his refusal to grant the mercy he himself was granted (Matthew 18:23-35).

Therefore, the *Compendium* (195) calls us to "the willingness to give oneself for the good of one's neighbor, beyond any individual or particular interest . . . so that humanity's journey will not be interrupted but remain open to present and future generations, all of them called together to share the same gift in solidarity."

## Jesus: The Perfection of Solidarity

Most of this teaching is both explicit and implicit in the natural law written on the heart, which tells us to do good and avoid evil. And it is perfected in the law known as the Golden Rule: Do to others what you would have them do to you. In the Kingdom of God, grace perfects nature and raises it to participate in the life of God himself. And so the *Compendium* (196) tells us that Solidarity reaches its climax in Jesus, the Son of Man, who joins himself to our humanity, becomes poor that we might become rich, and becomes sin for us that we might become the righteousness of God (2 Corinthians 5:21):

> *The unsurpassed apex of the perspective indicated here is the life of Jesus of Nazareth, the New Man, who is one with humanity even to the point of "death on a cross"* (Phil 2:8). In him it is always possible to recognize the living sign of that measureless and transcendent love of *God-with-us*, who takes on the infirmities of his people, walks with them, saves them and makes them one. In him and thanks to him, life in society too, despite all its contradictions and ambiguities, can be rediscovered as a place of life and hope, in that it is a sign of grace that is continuously offered to all and because it is an invitation to ever higher and more involved forms of sharing.

In the Kingdom of God, says the *Compendium* (196):

One's neighbor is then not only a human being

with his or her own rights and a fundamental equality with everyone else, but becomes the *living image* of God the Father, redeemed by the blood of Jesus Christ and placed under the permanent action of the Holy Spirit. One's neighbor must therefore be loved, even if an enemy, with the same love with which the Lord loves him or her; and for that person's sake one must be ready for sacrifice, even the ultimate one: to lay down one's life for the brethren (see 1 John 3:16).

That is why the Church—and each Christian—is bound to proclaim the gospel to the whole world: because the ultimate aim of working for the Common Good is that each person becomes a participant, not merely in social and economic life, but in the divine life: a member of the Body of Christ. Just as the point of Catholic economic teaching is that we become workers and owners of property as well as generous givers to the needs of others, so the point of salvation is that we become active participants in the work of God, not merely passive patients. So Paul teaches that God has given each member of the Body "varieties of gifts, but the same Spirit; and there are varieties of service, but the same Lord; and there are varieties of working, but it is the same God who inspires them all in every one. To each is given the manifestation of the Spirit for the common good" (1 Corinthians 12:4-7).

For our destiny is that each person become a full participant in the joy of glorifying God, loving neighbor as oneself in the splendor of the new heaven and the new earth where every member, as Paul teaches, is given his or her gifts

> for building up the body of Christ, until we all attain to the unity of the faith and of the knowledge of the Son of God, to mature manhood, to the measure of the stature of the fulness of Christ; so that we may no longer be children, tossed back and forth and carried about with every wind of doctrine, by the cunning of men, by their craftiness in deceitful wiles. Rather, speaking the truth in love, we are to grow up in every way into him who is the head, into Christ, from whom the whole body, joined and knit together by every joint with which it is supplied, when each part is working properly, makes bodily growth and upbuilds itself in love. (Ephesians 4:11–16)

## Questions:

1. What is meant by "Structures of Sin"? Can you think of some examples from history, current events, or from your personal experience?

2. How does the gospel challenge us to confront both our personal sins and the Structures of Sin we build? Can you think of some examples?

3. How do individuals and communities work together to reform Structures of Sin into communities of Solidarity?

# Chapter 9

# Afterword

*Every one then who hears these words of mine and does them will be like a wise man who built his house upon the rock; and the rain fell, and the floods came, and the winds blew and beat upon that house, but it did not fall, because it had been founded on the rock. And every one who hears these words of mine and does not do them will be like a foolish man who built his house upon the sand; and the rain fell, and the floods came, and the winds blew and beat against that house, and it fell; and great was the fall of it.* – Matthew 7:24-27

## Now What?

The social doctrine of the Church is, more than anything else in the deposit of faith, oriented toward action. In this book, we have discussed things that sometimes may seem theoretical. But in fact, they are eminently practical and boil down to this:

> But be doers of the word, and not hearers only, deceiving yourselves. For if any one is a hearer of the word and not a doer, he is like a man who observes his natural face in a mirror; for

he observes himself and goes away and at once forgets what he was like. But he who looks into the perfect law, the law of liberty, and perseveres, being no hearer that forgets but a doer that acts, he shall be blessed in his doing. (James 1:22-25)

Accordingly, as we finish this little primer on Catholic Social Teaching, it is vital that we do not simply put the book down and walk away, our heads full of a few rapidly fading ideas. We need to ask God how we can begin to put into practice the four pillars of Catholic Social Teaching so that we can better incarnate the work of the Holy Spirit in the world.

And this brings us to a paradox.

## The Thing about Catholic Social Teaching is That the Thing is Not About Catholic Social Teaching

There are certain things in life that you can only get by not trying to get them. In fact, in some cases, trying to get them guarantees that you will never get them. For instance, the worst way to become healthy is to spend your time obsessively focused on your health. The person who is constantly checking his pulse, taking his temperature, or fretting about every detail of his daily physiology is not going to become healthy. He is going to become a hypochondriac and ruin his health with perpetual worry.

Instead, the way to health is to focus on things higher than health alone: enjoyment of swimming, the pleasure of a walk on a fine day, cultivation of a taste for good food, a sane sleep schedule, a balance of work and leisure. Do these things and, as a general rule, health will come as well as a side benefit.

In short, as Jesus said, "Whoever would save his life will lose it; and whoever loses his life for my sake, he will save it" (Luke 9:24).

The same principle applies to Catholic Social Teaching. Though Jesus commands his disciples to care for other people's needs and to be quick to aid the least of these, he also cautions us that the needs of the human person and a healthy society cannot be fulfilled by focusing on social justice first:

> Therefore I tell you, do not be anxious about your life, what you shall eat or what you shall drink, nor about your body, what you shall put on. Is not life more than food, and the body more than clothing? Look at the birds of the air: they neither sow nor reap nor gather into barns, and yet your heavenly Father feeds them. Are you not of more value than they? And which of you by being anxious can add one cubit to his span of life? And why are you anxious about clothing? Consider the lilies of the field, how they grow; they neither toil nor spin; yet I tell you, even Solomon in all his glory was not clothed like one of these. But if God so clothes the grass of the field, which today is alive and tomorrow is thrown into the oven, will he not much more clothe you, O you of

little faith? Therefore do not be anxious, saying, "What shall we eat?" or "What shall we drink?" or "What shall we wear?" For the Gentiles seek all these things; and your heavenly Father knows that you need them all. But seek first his kingdom and his righteousness, and all these things shall be yours as well." (Matthew 6:25-33)

Set your mind on heavenly things and earthly things will come as a matter of course. Seek earth first and you won't even get that.

## Made for Heaven

This paradox arises from the fact that "creation was subjected to futility" (Romans 8:20). Sin is rooted in the attempt to find ultimate happiness in what is not God, which is like trying to go swimming while not getting wet. As a protection against such vanity, creation is so ordered that, as Augustine put it, "You have made us for Yourself, and our hearts are restless until they rest in You."[31] So in this world we can find only temporary pleasures and happiness, only fleeting joys and victories and progress. But any attempt to arrive at Heaven on earth is doomed. Indeed, the utopian temptation to create a perfect world without God—to "imagine there's no heaven, no hell below us, above us only sky," as John Lennon once sang—is the

---

31.    St. Augustine, *Confessions* I.1. Available on-line at http://www.newadvent.org/fathers/110101.htm as of June 30, 2018.

straightest road to the worst world-historical horrors the human race has ever devised.

That is why we must always seek first the Kingdom but seek to love our neighbor as a corollary, rather than treating social justice as the "real" part of Christianity and the "God stuff" as optional. As C.S. Lewis' devil Uncle Screwtape says in describing the strategy of Hell:

> About the general connection between Christianity and politics, our position is more delicate. Certainly we do not want men to allow their Christianity to flow over into their political life, for the establishment of anything like a really just society would be a major disaster. On the other hand we do want, and want very much, to make men treat Christianity as a means; preferably, of course, as a means to their own advancement, but, failing that, as a means to anything—even to social justice. The thing to do is to get a man at first to value social justice as a thing which the Enemy demands, and then work him on to the stage at which he values Christianity because it may produce social justice. For the Enemy will not be used as a convenience. Men or nations who think they can revive the Faith in order to make a good society might just as well think they can use the stairs of Heaven as a short cut to the nearest chemist's shop. Fortunately it is quite easy to coax humans round this little corner. Only today I have found a passage in a Christian

writer where he recommends his own version of Christianity on the ground that "only such a faith can outlast the death of old cultures and the birth of new civilisations". You see the little rift? "Believe this, not because it is true, but for some other reason." That's the game.[32]

If human beings are not a means to an end, still infinitely less is God himself a means to an end. And if we treat him as such, it will not be long before we treat human beings—made in his image—in the same way. The second greatest commandment—to love one's neighbor as one's self—must always be obeyed if we are to obey the first and greatest commandment—to love God. But the first and greatest commandment may never be treated as irrelevant or subordinate to the second.

## Some Practical Steps

As we have already seen, much of Catholic Social Teaching is already being lived out by ordinary people going to work, taking care of their families, volunteering with local mediating institutions, or reading their voter pamphlets thoughtfully and trying to do the right thing. The Church certainly does not want us to undo the good you and I are already doing in our day-to-day lives. Most of us are already doing many good things, often because we

---

32. C.S. Lewis, *The Screwtape Letters*. Available on-line at http://www.samizdat.qc.ca/arts/lit/PDFs/ScrewtapeLetters_CSL.pdf as of February 21, 2020.

have become participants in structures of Solidarity that our civilization built for us before we were born. We join the Boy Scouts, or help out at the St. Vincent de Paul Society food bank, or get involved in some charity at the office, or argue for a living wage, or join a union, or protest at a local abortion clinic, or rally to stop mistreatment of refugees, or help the Sierra Club, stand against racism, or do any of a host of other things because our family, church, synagogue, mosque, political group, circle of friends, or other group we identify with has taught us that this is the Done Thing, so we do it. That's good, but as George MacDonald once observed, "God is easy to please, but hard to satisfy." He always calls us further up and further in.

This means that the first practical step is always to begin where you are, not where you are not. C.S Lewis gives some remarkably simple advice about how to do that:

> Remember the story in the *Imitation*, how the Christ on the crucifix suddenly spoke to the monk who was so anxious about his salvation and said "If you knew that all was well, what would you, to-day, do, or stop doing?" When you have found the answer, do it or stop doing it.[33]

The next practical step is to *challenge* ourselves with some aspect of Catholic Social Teaching that pushes us out of our comfort zone. When the Rich Young Man

---

33. C.S. Lewis, *Letters to An American Lady* (Grand Rapids: Eerdmans, 1967), 74.

came to Jesus and asked what he had to do to be saved, Jesus told him to keep the commandments (see Luke 18:18-23). When the Rich Young Man replied, "All this I have observed from my youth," Jesus immediately challenged him: "One thing you still lack. Sell all that you have and distribute to the poor, and you will have treasure in heaven; and come, follow me." The point of the story is that Jesus demanded that he confront an idol more important to him than the eternal life he wanted. We need to confront our idols so that we too are free to follow Jesus and do the right thing. Our idols are typically some combination of money, pleasure, power, and/or honor. And what we fear to confront often provides a clue about what we need to confront.

There are myriad ways to start. One is to pray over the Corporal and Spiritual Works of Mercy and ask the Holy Spirit to challenge you to try something new. These Works of Mercy are an ancient part of the Church's tradition addressing both the physical and spiritual needs of the human person.[34]

The Corporal Works of Mercy call us to feed the hungry, give drink to the thirsty, clothe the naked, shelter the homeless, visit the sick and imprisoned, ransom the captive, and bury the dead.

The Spiritual Works of Mercy call us to instruct the ignorant, counsel the doubtful, admonish the sinner, bear

---

34. For more information on the Corporal and Spiritual Works of Mercy, see my book *The Work of Mercy: Being the Hands and Heart of Christ* (Cincinnati: Franciscan Media, 2011).

patiently those who wrong us, forgive offenses, comfort the afflicted, and pray for the living and the dead.

Perhaps you know of a need involving one of these Works of Mercy such as a call to help with your local food bank. You could help feed the hungry. Or maybe you saw a conversation on-line in which somebody was trying to understand something about the Church's teaching and was looking for a resource. You could try instructing the ignorant by referring them to the *Catechism*. Maybe the footnote in this book about the fight for slave-free chocolate struck you. You could check out that link and get involved in the Church's work of ransoming the captive. The idea is to stretch yourself into a new area of care for the Common Good.

## Vocation and Charism

Of course, not everybody is cut out for every calling. As Christians we have to walk a line between lapsing into merely living in our comfort zone and rushing off into our area of complete incompetence. Sometimes we simply do not have the gifts or the resources to fill a need. My parish finance council might be crying out for an accountant to organize the books, but I know nothing about accounting and finance. On the other hand, you might be just the person for such work and have a real knack for it.

So discernment of our path to growth has to take into account the virtue of prudence as we seek to stretch ourselves. We should take stock of our spiritual gifts (aka "charisms") and talents as clues to the direction in which we might extend ourselves into the Works of Mercy. I may not be able to balance complex books, but is there a way I could be more generous to that homeless guy I walk past every day? Suppose I shake his hand and talk to him instead of hurrying past? What if I buy him a meal or see if there is a shelter in the area where he can stay during a cold snap? Suppose I figure out how to get him a tent? What if I resolve to challenge myself this week to treat every person who comes to me as if that one were Jesus? I might find myself on the path to helping the homeless community.

Charisms are valuable diagnostic tools because, in the words of Sherry Weddell, "If you are called, you have been gifted and if you have been gifted, you are called." As she also notes, "A vocation is a work of love to which you have been called." What that work may be is our task to discern.[35]

## Maximalism vs. Minimum Daily Adult Thinking

As will quickly be seen, it is not a problem to find things to do. Virtually any place you turn you can find ways of contributing to the Common Good and seeking to further the Dignity of the Human Person. Google "contribute to the Common Good" and you will (as of this writing) find 4,140,000 links. As Paul says, "Whatever you do, in word or deed, do everything in the name of the

---

35. I highly recommend you check out all the excellent books by Sherry Weddell, beginning with *Forming Intentional Disciples*, for insightful and practical wisdom on how discern your charisms and fulfil your vocation in the service of the Kingdom of God and the Common Good.

Lord Jesus, giving thanks to God the Father through him" (Colossians 3:17). The main issue for most of us is the *way* in which we approach it.

What I mean is this: many people approach the question of obedience to Christ with a minimalist legal mindset. You may have seen it in action: "How do I keep the rules so that I am technically OK with God? How many things do I have to do? What can I get away with not doing?"

This mindset is insufficient because it is rooted in fear, not love. It sees God as a taskmaster who makes us jump through hoops and ourselves as jailhouse lawyers haggling over the cost. What God seeks, however, is a "cheerful giver" (2 Corinthians 9:7). This does not refer only to financial generosity, but to a proactive spirit that seeks to obey God out of *love*. It is the difference between somebody who asks on his wedding day, "How often do I have to kiss my wife for it to count as a marriage?" and the one who cannot wait to be with his love and is busily thinking of ways to pour out his life for the Beloved. To such a spirit, rules are not to be fastidiously observed out of fear, but transcended out of love. The one who loves his wife understands that, as a rule, a loving husband will kiss his wife several times a day. But he would laugh at the notion of actually keeping count to fill a tally. It should be the same with our love for God and neighbor.

## Forming Habits of Virtue

Developing that habit of generous love for God and neighbor takes practice and training because selfishness is our normal fallen disposition. So Paul tells us:

> But I say, walk by the Spirit, and do not gratify the desires of the flesh. For the desires of the flesh are against the Spirit, and the desires of the Spirit are against the flesh; for these are opposed to each other, to prevent you from doing what you would. But if you are led by the Spirit you are not under the law. Now the works of the flesh are plain: immorality, impurity, licentiousness, idolatry, sorcery, enmity, strife, jealousy, anger, selfishness, dissension, party spirit, envy, drunkenness, carousing, and the like. I warn you, as I warned you before, that those who do such things shall not inherit the kingdom of God. But the fruit of the Spirit is love, joy, peace, patience, kindness, goodness, faithfulness, gentleness, self-control; against such there is no law. And those who belong to Christ Jesus have crucified the flesh with its passions and desires. (Galatians 5:16-24)

Consequently, we are required, on the one hand, to ask God for the grace to help do the works of the Spirit while simultaneously buckling down to deliberately form what are called "habits of virtue." As Paul says, "Work out your own salvation with fear and trembling; for God is at work in you, both to will and to work for his good pleasure" (Philippians 2:12-13). This makes clear the incarnational nature of what we are to do as we cooperate with God to order the world for the Dignity of the Human Person and the Common Good in Solidarity with the human race. The first part sounds like we do everything while the second part makes clear that God is acting through us by our free choice.

And as we form habits of virtue, those habits become second nature, just like learning to say "Please" and "Thank you" when we were small. Such habits of virtue are not binding or dull, but liberating. Just as the bicyclist's initial wobbly attempts free him (with some practice) to not have to think at all about operating a bike as he takes a ride on a beautiful day, so our practice of the habits of virtue free us so that we can focus on all sorts of good things.

And so, the ships C.S. Lewis spoke of become seaworthy and in good order. And because of this, we become better able to sail in formation as good citizens, employers, workers, and family members. We learn to study that we might do interesting and fulfilling work for the Common Good. We learn courtesy so that we can have friendships and rewarding relationships. We learn habits of diligent work, or prayer, or attentive citizenship, or attention to others so that we can grow into people who use our gifts not only for our own happiness but for the community and all those we love. That is how we put the principles of Catholic Social Teaching into practice so that we can sail in formation.

Finally, as Catholics, we believe that this struggle to live in a community of love is not simply a form of crowd control or sociology with smells and bells. The fleet is going somewhere. As Scripture says, "Here we have no lasting city, but we seek the city which is to come" (Hebrews 13:14). The fleet is not designed to sail and then sink, but to take us to that place where all of our practice in being decent citizens, good workers, loving family, and gifted members of the human community bears fruit in our becoming saints. Scripture promises that our struggle to live in love in this life will make us, by the grace of God, into divinized men and women enjoying a common life in God. It is not some dewy glade of isolated contemplation, not some white void of transcendence, not some silent place all alone with God, but a *city*—the New Jerusalem—that the New Testament offers as the great image of the Age to Come. "Myriads of myriads" will be there (see Revelation 5:11). Indeed, they are already there and more are coming daily, for we have already "come to Mount Zion and to the city of the living God, the heavenly Jerusalem, and to innumerable angels in festal gathering, and to the assembly of the first-born who are enrolled in heaven, and to a judge who is God of all, and to the spirits of just men made perfect, and to Jesus, the mediator of a new covenant" (Hebrews 12:22-24).

So let us study diligently and practice earnestly the principles of Catholic Social Teaching, not simply that we may have earthly happiness, civil order, healthier families, and a more just world—good as these things are. Let us seek to tune our instruments in this life so that, on That Day, we may take our place in the Great Symphony where "the dwelling of God is with men. He will dwell with them, and they shall be his people, and God himself will be with them; he will wipe away every tear from their eyes, and death shall be no more, neither shall there be mourning nor crying nor pain any more, for the former things have passed away" (Revelation 21:3-4).

## Questions:

1. How does Jesus' command to "seek first the Kingdom of Heaven, challenge the ways in which you prioritize your approach to life?

2. How does Jesus' insistence that obedience to the second great commandment is the only way to prove your obedience to the first great commandment challenge how you prioritize your approach to life?

3. What first practical step can you take today to bring your life into closer conformity with the will of Jesus?

# Bibliography

Thomas Aquinas. *Catena Aurea: Commentary on the Four Gospels: St. Luke.* Seattle: Veritatis Splendor Publications, 2012.

Augustine. *Confessions.* Translated by Henry Chadwick. Oxford: Oxford University Press, 2008.

Budziszewski, J. *What We Can't Not Know.* San Francisco: Ignatius, 2011.

*Catechism of the Catholic Church.* Rome: Libreria Editrice Vaticana, 2019.

*Compendium of the Social Doctrine of the Church.* Rome: Libreria Editrice Vaticana, 2004.

Chesterton, G.K. *Orthodoxy.* New York: Open Road Media, 2015.

Donne, John. *The Complete English Poems*, edited by A. Smith. London: Penguin, 2004.

*Documents of Vatican II,* edited by Austin Flannery. Collegeville: Liturgical Press, 1996.

Hopkins, Gerard Manley. *The Complete Poems of Gerard Manley Hopkins,* edited with notes by Robert Bridges. Overland Park: Digireads.com, 2018.

*The Ignatius Bible: Revised Standard Version – Second Catholic Edition.* San Francisco: Ignatius, 2009.

Ivereigh, Austen. *Wounded Shepherd: Pope Francis and His Struggle to Convert the Catholic Church.* New York: Macmillan, 2019.

Lewis, C. S. *Mere Christianity.* New York: HarperCollins, 2009.

—*Letters to An American Lady.* New York: HarperOne, 2014.

—*The Screwtape Letters.* New York: HarperCollins, 2009.

—*The Weight of Glory.* New York: HarperCollins, 2009.

—*The World's Last Night and Other Essays.* New York: HarperOne, 2017.

Miller, Arthur. *Death of a Salesman.* New York: Viking, 1996.

Pope John Paul II. *Ecclesia in America.* Boston: St. Paul Books, 1999.

Weddell, Sherry. *Forming Intentional Disciples: The Path to Knowing and Following Jesus.* Huntington: Our Sunday Visitor, 2012.

# Suggested Reading

One useful place to dig deeper is to read the Church's social encyclicals. They are, at one and the same time, responses to contemporary events as well as rooted in the timeless wisdom of the Tradition. Because of this, they show the way in which the Tradition is both unchanging and developing. Tradition has basic principles as a body has unbending bones, yet it is flexible and lithe, as a body uses the strength of its skeleton not to be rigid, but to dance in a thousand beautiful and supple ways as the situation requires to meet human need. To read these encyclicals is to watch the Church navigate the waters of the past century from the rise of the modern capitalist state through Depression, Global War, Cold War, and on to the challenges of postmodern global civilization we now face. All of them are available at www.vatican.va.

Leo XIII, *Rerum Novarum* (On Capital and Labor), May 15, 1891.

Pius XI, *Quadragesimo Anno* (After Forty Years) - On Reconstruction of the Social Order, May 15, 1931 - the 40th anniversary of *Rerum Novarum*.

John XXIII, *Mater et Magistra* (On Christianity and Social Progress), May 15, 1961 - the 60th anniversary of *Rerum Novarum*.

— *Pacem in Terris* (Peace on Earth), April 11, 1963 - on Establishing Universal Peace in Truth, Justice, Charity, and Liberty.

Paul VI, *Populorum Progressio* (On the Development of Peoples), March 27, 1967.

John Paul II, *Laborem Exercens* (On Human Work), September 14, 1981 - the 90th anniversary of *Rerum Novarum.*

—*Sollicitudo Rei Socialis* (20th Anniversary of Populorum Progressio), December 30, 1987.

—*Centesimus Annus* (The Hundredth Year), May 1, 1991 - the 100th anniversary of *Rerum Novarum.*

—*Evangelium Vitae* (The Gospel of Life), March 25, 1995.

—*Fides et Ratio* (Faith and Reason), September 14, 1998.

Benedict XVI, *Deus Caritas Est* (God Is Love), December 15, 2005.

—*Caritas in Veritate* (Charity in Truth), June 29, 2009.

Francis, *Laudato Si'* (On Care for Our Common Home), May 24, 2015.

In addition, here are a few texts (by no means exhaustive) that allow an explorer to dip his or her toes into this rapidly developing work of the Church in the world:

Boyle, S.J., Gregory. *Barking to the Choir: The Power of Radical Kinship.* New York: Simon & Schuster, 2017.

—*Tattoos on the Heart: The Power of Boundless Compassion.* New York: Simon & Schuster, 2010.

*Catholic Social Teaching: A Volume of Scholarly Essays,* Gerard V. Bradley, E. Christian Brugger, editors. Cambridge: Cambridge University Press, 2019.

Day, Dorothy. *The Long Loneliness.* New York: HarperOne, 2017.

— *The Reckless Way of Love: Notes on Following Jesus.* Farmington: Plough, 2017.

Himes, Kenneth R. *Responses to 101 Questions on Catholic Social Teaching.* Mahwah: Paulist Press, 2001.

— *Modern Catholic Social Teaching: Commentaries and Interpretations.* Washington, D.C.: Georgetown University Press, 2005.

Keenan, James. *Moral Wisdom: Lessons and Texts from the Catholic Tradition.* Lanham: Rowman & Littlefield, 2016.

Maurin, Peter. *Easy Essays.* Eugene: Wipf & Stock, 2010.

McGreevy, John T. *Catholicism and American Freedom: A History.* New York: W.W. Norton & Co., 2004.

McIntyre, Alasdair. *After Virtue: A Study in Moral Theory.* South Bend: Notre Dame, 2007.

Romero, Oscar. *The Scandal of Redemption: When God Liberates the Poor, Saves Sinners, and Heals Nations.* Farmington: Plough, 2018.

Schwindt, Daniel. *Catholic Social Teaching: A New Synthesis (Rerum Novarum to Laudato Si').* McPherson: Agnus Dei Publishing, 2015.

Shea, Mark P. *The Work of Mercy: Being the Hands and Heart of Christ.* Cincinnati: Franciscan Media, 2011.

## On Video

Jesus often taught by means of story. The medium of film is often a good way to learn about truths of the gospel's social teaching, as well as about those who have lived those truths and applied them creatively.

*A Man for All Seasons*: Robert Bolt's superbly well-written and acted story of Thomas More's confrontation with the state vs. the claims of conscience.

*Amazing Grace*: The story of English Christian William Wilberforce and his triumphant struggle to abolish the British slave trade.

*Bella*: Winner of the People's Choice Award at the Toronto Film Festival and a fine celebration of the dignity of human life and love.

*Dead Man Walking*: The story of Sr. Helen Prejean's ministry to death row prisoners, dramatizing well the Church's opposition to the death penalty.

*Juno*: A comedy that affirms the Catholic ethos of openness to life.

*The Mayo Clinic: Faith–Hope–Science*: Documentarian Ken Burns' masterful account of Catholics nuns working with dedicated physicians to create one of the greatest healing institutions in the history of the world.

*The Mission*: A beautiful, heartbreaking story of the suppression of Jesuit missionaries in 18th century South America.

*Molokai*: The story of St. Damien of Molokai, who went to live with the lepers and care for them in a time when no one would.

*Of Gods and Men*: A powerful story of love and courage about Algerian monks who lived in harmony with their Muslim community until their martyrdom by Islamist fanatics.

*One Child Nation*: 2019 Sundance U.S. Grand Jury Prize-winning documentary examines the devastating consequences of China's One-Child Policy through the stories of those who lived through it.

*Revolution of the Heart: The Dorothy Day Story*: Martin Doblmeier's fine documentary on one of the great practitioners of the Church's social teaching from the 20th century.

*Romero*: The gripping story of saint and martyr Oscar Romero.

# Index

# About the Author

Mark P. Shea is author and co-author of numerous books, including the *New York Times* best-seller *A Guide to the Passion: 100 Questions About The Passion of the Christ* (Ascension), *By What Authority?: An Evangelical Discovers Catholic Tradition* (Ignatius), *Mary, Mother of the Son, This is My Body: An Evangelical Discovers the Real Presence* (Christendom), *Making Senses Out of Scripture: Reading the Bible as the First Christians Did* (Basilica), *The Work of Mercy: Being the Heart and Hands of Christ* (Servant), *Salt and Light: The Commandments, the Beatitudes, and a Joyful Life* (Servant), and *The Heart of Catholic Prayer: Rediscovering the Our Father and the Hail Mary*. He has contributed numerous articles to many magazines. In addition, Mark is an internationally known speaker on the Catholic Faith. He can be found online at his blog "Stumbling Toward Heaven" and at his Patreon page. He lives near Seattle with his wife, Janet, and their family.